SEARCHING FOR GOD

PART II

A Journey into the Heart of the Divine Mother

by DAYALU (TED ZEFF, Ph.D.)

SHIVA PUBLISHING
San Ramon, California

SEARCHING FOR GOD PARTII:
A Journey into the Heart
of the Divine Mother

PUBLISHED BY:
SHIVA PUBLISHING
P.O. Box 613
San Ramon, CA 94583

Cover Design by Alfred Rordame iv

ISBN 0-9660745-1-3

Permissions

Permission to reprint excerpts from the following is gratefully acknowledged:

Awaken Children, Volumes I-VII; Dialogues with Mata Amritanandamayi , by Swami Amritaswarupananda. Copyright 1995 by M.A. Center. Reprinted by permission.

Bhjajanamritam: Devotional Songs Vol.3, San Ramon, CA. M.A. Center, 1996. Reprinted by permission.

Cosmic Chants, by Paramahansa Yogananda. Copyright 1938 by Self- Realization Fellowship. Reprinted by permission of Self-Realization Fellowship.

Forgiveness/Loving the Inner Child, audio tape by Louise Hay, Santa Monica, Ca. 1989. Reprinted by permission.

Dedication

This book is dedicated to

The Divine Mother

Mata Amritanandamayi

I humbly bow at your lotus feet

Acknowledgements

This book could not have been written without the excellent editing skills of Swami Amritaswarupananda, Shakti (Pete) Eriksson and Timothy Conway. I want to thank the souls of my parents, Dave and Sylvia Zeff, who taught me the importance of seeking spiritual truths; Finally, I want to thank all the devotees who allowed me to share their experiences with Ammachi.

TABLE OF CONTENTS

Come quickly, darling children, you who are the essence of Om. Break away from all the shackles that you have carefully nurtured, and become one with the sacred syllable Om.

*

Give up self-indulgence and make your self-control a role model for the whole world.

*

Let the contemplation of the Self take deep roots within you. The ecstatic inner experiences of truth and dharma will blossom in due course.

PREFACE

In 1997 I wrote my first book about my experiences with my be-loved guru, Mata Amritanandamayi, which included stories from 1988 to 1997. *Searching For God Part II* is an account of my spiritual experiences with Amma from 1997 to 2001. Since I first met Ammachi in 1988, I've recorded all of my special experiences with the Holy Mother. Each word uttered by Amma is like a teaching from the scriptures that the devotee could spend a long time pondering like a Zen koan. However, the power of maya is so strong that I am continuously shocked how easily I've been able to forget all the spiritually uplifting experiences that I've had in the presence of this great saint. I encourage devotees to record all of their special encounters with Mother and to frequently review all the blessings that Mother has continuously showered upon them.

If there is anything in this book which uplifts you spiritually, it is coming from Amma. However, if there is anything that you find offensive, it is due to my ego. My sincere wish is that this book may stimulate the reader to grow closer to Amma and dive deeply into her eternal bliss.

*

This book includes Sanskrit words that have been italicized and defined the first time they appear in the book. Definitions are also listed in the glossary. The quotes dispersed throughout this book that are in bold print are taken from *Awaken Children, Volumes I-VII; Dialogues with Mata Amritanandamayi* and from *Bhajanamritam* Volume *III: Devotional Songs of Mata Amritanandamayi*.

*

The word Amma is Malayalam (the language spoken in the state of Kerala, India) for Mother. She is also referred to as Ammachi (respected Mother), Mata Amritanandmayi (the mother of divine bliss), Holy Mother and Divine Mother.

*

The answers to the questions that Ammachi has given to the author were meant just for him and the reader should not assume that Amma would give the reader the same answers.

An Introduction to Amma

Prior to Amma's first world tour in 1987, she was virtually unknown outside of the state of Kerala in India. Each year Ammachi's popularity has grown as more people recognize her true greatness; that she is one with the Divine Mother of the Universe. Amma now has millions of devotees throughout the world from India to Brazil; from Canada to Italy; from Costa Rica to Australia; from Kuwait to Japan.

Ammachi's service to humanity has been praised in such distinguished periodicals as the New York Times, The Washington Post and the San Francisco Chronicle. She has appeared on American television on programs like the "Today Show," touching an audience of millions throughout North America. She has been the focus of numerous television interviews on major networks in such cities as Seattle, Los Angeles, Chicago, Dallas and New York. Amma has been invited to speak at the United Nations in New York on two separate occasions as well as at the Parliament of World Religions in Chicago.

Ammachi's work has blossomed into an international organization engaged in many spiritual and charitable activities. Mother's compassion for the poor resulted in her assuming responsibility for a financially troubled orphanage near her Indian ashram. More than four hundred children were starving and lived in filthy buildings on the verge of collapse. Ashram residents cleaned and improved the facility. Electricity and plumbing were installed and the children were fed nourishing food. With the material basics taken care of, a comprehensive educational and spiritual program was instituted.

Amrita Institute of Technology

Mother also has been involved in starting vocational training centers; creating hospices for the terminally ill; building houses for the poor as well as distributing food and clothing to the underprivileged. It was Amma's wish that a multi-specialty charitable hospital in Cochin, Southern India be created. The 800 bed hospital, which opened in 1997 gives comprehensive medical services to all in need regardless of race or religion. The Prime Minister of India, Atal Behari Vajpayee, attended the inauguration of the hospital. In addition, Amma has motivated hundreds of devotees in cities throughout the United States to feed the poor in a program called Mother's Kitchen.

How did an unknown, short lady from a poor fishing village in Southern India become a world-renown spiritual leader of millions throughout the world in less than a decade?

Mata Amritanandamayi is the embodiment of unconditional love, devoted to the service of all humanity. People from all walks of life seek out Mother, as she is affectionately called. She receives everyone in the same loving way, regardless of one's religious faith or non-belief. She welcomes all alike, from the wealthy executive to the leprous beggar, from the newborn infant to the wrinkled old man, from the hostile detractor to the ardent admirer. As an untiring servant of all people, her life is dedicated solely to removing the suffering of humanity. No one's concerns are insignificant to her.

Ammachi's motherly affection is a soothing balm to all who come to her. Taking each person to herself without reservation, she is like a mother with children, bringing solace and peace of mind to all. Her touch is so deeply moving that many burst into tears as they experience the radiance of her divine love and compassion. She teaches by the example of her own life and conveys the highest spiritual truths in the simplest language. She has infused devotion to God, love for fellow beings and the spirit of selfless service into the hearts of millions.

Sudhamani (Ammachi's birth name) was born September 27, 1953 to an extremely poor but pious family in the lush state of Kerela on the Southwest coast of India. She is the fourth of eight surviving children. At her birth, her family was perplexed at the infant Sudhamani's dark blue complexion. Doctors ruled out disease and the blue hue on Sudhamani's skin gradually disappeared over the course of her first year. However, her family members' aversion to this incident marked the beginning of years of ridicule and abuse. Although as a child she underwent many severe hardships and encountered many obstacles, she sought solace in God.

Adding tn the family' s bewilderment was Sudhamani's early mastery of Malayalam, the region's local language. She began speaking at six months, and by age two; Sudhamani was singing songs and prayers in praise of *Krishna* without having received any formal instruction. At the age of five, she began composing songs of deep devotional significance. Her enchanting, soulful singing became well known throughout the village.

Amma has said, "From childhood I had an intense love of the Divine Name. I would repeat the Lord's Name incessantly with every breath, and a constant flow of divine thoughts was kept in my mind no matter the place where I was or the work I was doing."

As the years passed, Sudhamani spent all of her free time immersed in meditation, longing for Krishna. People frequently found her sitting with eyes closed, softly singing to God with tears streaming down her cheeks. Although her family and many of the neighbors were religious, they did not understand Sudhamani's intense spiritual moods.

However, childhood friends readily gravitated to Sudhamani's playful, joyous, charismatic nature. After finishing her chores, she would tell friends spiritual stories about the playful child Krishna. At these times, her playmates would sing devotional songs that were composed by Sudhamani.

Required to work long hours in the service of her family, she could not continue attending school beyond the fourth grade. In addition to looking after all the family household chores, she served the elderly, poor, and sick in her seaside village as if they were members of her own family. She would often remove food and clothing from her family's home and distribute them to those who were poorer than herself. One day, not finding anything else, she gave away her mother's only gold bangle to a poor, starving man. She received a severe beating when her father found out, yet she was happy that she could relieve someone's suffering.

Eventually Sudhamani was locked out of her house. When sympathetic local women tried to bring her food and take care of her, they were sent away by the family. Some of the local villagers who could not understand her state of divine bliss ridiculed her by throwing stones at her and placing thorns where she walked. Yet despite all these abuses,

Sudhamani remained undisturbed, oblivious to the harassment and physical conditions. She slept outdoors; the sand was her bed, the stars her blanket and the moon her light. Animals came to feed her. In fact, a dog was seen bringing food packets to her in his mouth; and a cow stood near her so that she could drink from its udder.

One day in September 1975, Sudhamani overheard a family singing devotional songs to Krishna. She was immediately overtaken by divine bliss as her appearance spontaneously transformed into the features and movements of Krishna. During the transformation, her skin hue became more blue like that of Krishna. This event marked her first manifestation of *Krishna Bhava*, the Divine mood of Krishna.

Many people assumed that Krishna had temporarily taken possession of Sudhamani in order to bless them, and news of this rapidly spread throughout the local villages. Skeptics abounded, and one of them demanded that Sudhamani perform a miracle as proof that she was indeed Krishna. She replied, "It is not my intention to show miracles. My goal is to inspire people with the desire for liberation through *realization* (the state of complete identity with God). Miracles are illusory. That is not the essential principle behind spirituality. Not only that, once a miracle is shown you will desire and demand to see it again and again. I am not here to create desire but to remove it."

Yet out of compassion towards the villagers and to inspire them with faith, she asked one of the skeptics to bring a cistern of water. After a portion was distributed to the devotees, Sudhamani told the skeptic to dip his finger in what remained. To everyone's amazement, the water had turned to milk and the urn was full. The milk was then distributed among the crowd. Another skeptic was called up by Sudhamani, and he was instructed to dip his finger into the remaining milk. It was immediately transformed into a pudding made from milk, bananas, sugar and raisins. This too was distributed to the hundreds of people assembled. This event created a vast change in the minds of the people. From that day on large crowds gathered around her.

On another occasion, a devotee of Ammachi brought her an oil lamp for the little temple in which she received devotees, but her elder brother who felt she was bringing shame on the family, smashed it. Amma then asked the devotees to bring shells into which water was poured, and a wick was placed in each. She asked the people there to light them and the light from these shells lasted the entire night.

However, as the crowds grew larger to receive Sudhamani's blessings, the vehemence toward her behavior grew. An opposition movement felt threatened by her for not following the traditional role of a woman in India of marrying, bearing children and staying at home. They ridiculed her and plotted her death.

During Krishna Bhava the devotees would offer Sudhamani milk to drink. One day an atheist milk vendor secretly added poison to the milk that a devotee bought to offer to Sudamani. Although she knew the milk was poisoned, she did not want to upset the devotee so she drank it. Sudhamani continued the program until every devotee received her blessing.

One day while Sudhamani was sitting alone in a meditative mood, a beautiful orb of brilliant light appeared before her. As she looked on in wonder, the Divine Mother emerged in an exquisitely beautiful form and then suddenly disappeared along with the light. This vision left Sudhamani with an intense desire to see the Divine Mother again. After many days of meditation and crying out, the Divine Mother at last reappeared and merged in her. Following this experience, Sudhamani withdrew herself from everything and everyone, and remained immersed in the intense inner bliss of God-Consciousness.

However, suddenly one day she heard a voice from within her say, "I am in all as the One Essence and do not have a particular abode. It is to give solace to the suffering humanity that you have come into this world and not merely for enjoying Divine Bliss. Therefore, worship Me by showing mankind the way back to Me." This was a turning point in Sudhamani's life. The following days found her identified with the loving Divine Mother and it was from this time onwards that people began calling Sudhamani "Mother" or "Ammachi."

Once she heard this call from the Divine Mother, approximately six months after the beginning of Krishna Bhava, Ammachi began manifesting *Devi Bhava*, the mood of the Divine Mother. Ammachi has said, "All the deities represent the infinite aspects of the One Supreme Being, which exist within us as well. A divine personality can manifest any one of them by mere will for the good of the world. Devi Bhava is the manifestation of the Eternal Feminine, the Creatrix; the active principle of the Impersonal Absolute.

"It should be remembered that all objects having a name or form are mere mental projections. Why should a doctor wear a white coat or a policeman a uniform and cap? All these are merely external aids meant to create a certain impression. In a like manner, Ammachi dons the garb of Devi in order to give strength to the devotional attitude of the people. The Universal Spirit that is in me is also within you. If you can realize that Indivisible Principle that is ever shining in you, you will become one with That."

Since 1981 the Holy Mother has been disseminating spiritual knowledge to thousands of spiritual aspirants who have come to study with her, training them with practical spiritual discipline. She has stated that the greatest of all blessings is to rouse an aspirant to the glory of the divinity within.

Chapter I

The Omniscient Guru

"The omniscient Guru will gradually take the disciple to the goal. Attachment to the Guru's form supported by the awareness of his omniscience and all-pervasiveness is the perfect attitude. The Guru's sole intention is to improve the disciple. The Guru will observe each and every action of the disciple but the disciple will not know it."

The 93rd name of Amma: The one who sees all the actions of the disciple

Amma remembers everything that the millions of devotees ask her each year. Mother told the devotees in a recent satsang, "Do you know how many letters arrive on any single day? Thousands; in many languages. There are one thousand residents, and five hundred computer students. There will be at least three to five hundred daily letters from them. Then there are letters from devotees who come for *darshan* (audience of a holy person). If there are ten to fifteen thousand people, then Mother will receive at least three thousand letters."

A friend of mine, Chaitanya, asked Mother in 1988 if he could go to India to be with Amma. She responded, "I'll let you know when you're supposed to come."

Seven years later in 1995, he once again asked her if he could come to India. Mother's omniscient response was, "Don't you remember? I told you that I would let you know when it will be the right time for you to come."

During the very end of one morning program during the summer U.S. tour, the fans had not been used since it was a cool day. Since there were only a few more people to be blessed, Chaitanya thought, "I'll put the fans away now since they won't be used." At that very moment Mother asked him to turn the fans on letting him know that Mother is aware of all his thoughts.

In 1991 I sent a question with a friend who was going to see Amma in New York. I had asked her about whether I should move to Albuquerque to study ayurveda. She responded clearly, "No."

The following year, over 100,000 questions later, I sent a note with another friend asking Mother if it was o.k. for me to come to India to see her. Her response really startled me. "He didn't have to ask this question. It's not like when he asked about moving to Albuquerque. He had to ask that since he didn't know if it was best for his spiritual growth. I think he'll understand what I'm referring to. You can't go wrong if you're going to see the Divine Mother."

During each program many people have the opportunity to hand Mother *prasad* (a sacred offering of chocolate kisses and flower petals which she gives to everyone when she blesses them). An ashram resident, Shakti, missed his ten-minute prasad shift. Although no one told Mother who was scheduled to give prasad, when it was turn for Shakti's shift, Amma kept looking around asking, "Where's Shakti?"

In June of 1997 Mother called me up for darshan. The night before I had been visiting Shakti in the hospital when he was experiencing a difficult time undergoing chemotherapy. He mentioned that he was feeling very sad that instead of being with Amma at the San Ramon ashram, he was suffering in the hospital not feeling connected to Mother. The two of us were alone in his hospital room when he became really sick and vomited. However, later that evening he began to feel much better physically. Mother looked at me when I went up for darshan the following morning and asked me, "Yesterday Shakti vomited in the hospital, but then felt better?"

She let me know that she was with Shakti in the hospital blessing and healing him.

Many years earlier Shakti experienced Mother's grace in another rather dramatic way. In the early morning of the last day of programs in the Bay Area, Amma was pacing back and forth stating that something bad was going to happen to one of her children that day.

The final program at the San Ramon ashram had ended and the devotees were breaking down the temple in preparation for packing things up and traveling to Los Angeles. Shakti climbed an old extension ladder to take down a banner that was hanging from the top of the ceiling, which was approximately three stories high. The ladder was not completely secure on the slippery, cement floor and slid out from underneath him. Suddenly, he fell thirty feet, landing on his head and arm when he hit the concrete floor far below. One horrified observer remembered that she could literally see his head bouncing off the floor. The shocked devotees in the temple came running toward him fearing the worst. A nurse happened to be nearby and she was surprised that he was still conscious. He was rushed to the hospital by the paramedics, but miraculously only suffered a broken arm.

Shakti later described the accident, saying it felt as if Amma had put an invisible net beneath him to break the fall. However, he still had to go through the karmic experience. The Holy Mother later told him that astrologically he was destined to die that day, but through divine grace, he survived. Amma said that the Universal Mother had absorbed his karma that day and what would have been certain death became a minor accident. The banner that Shakti was taking down was the symbol of "*Sri Chakra,*" which represents the Universal Mother. This was the last thing he grabbed onto for support as he began plummeting toward the concrete floor.

However, while Shakti was recuperating in the hospital, at one point the pain became unbearable. He was in such intense agony even after he was given a large dose of morphine, he cried out to Amma for help. All of the sudden, he felt himself rising above his body, where Amma appeared and gently caressed him. A moment later he returned to his body and he was miraculously pain-free. When he went to Santa Fe a few weeks later, he excitedly began to relate the incident to Amma, and Mother simply responded, "Yes, yes, I know."

In another story illustrating Mother's omniscience, a devotee named Udar was diagnosed with lymphoma right after Mother left San Ramon in the summer of 2001. When he flew to Boston to see Mother during the last Devi Bhava, he cried to her about the catastrophic diagnosis. She told him to put his head on her shoulder and he noticed that Mother was crying too. He was so touched that the Goddess Devi would weep with him for his pain that he was in awe of Mother's pure unconditional compassion.

At that moment he could literally feel Mother's grace entering through his mouth and touching every cell in his body. Mother usually instructs devotees with cancer to follow the doctor's recommendations for allopathic treatment. However, she told Udar to try a holistic approach for healing his cancer. Several months later the doctors were going to begin aggressively treating the cancer since the specialists had recommended traditional allopathic treatment. The doctors were dumbfounded when the lab test miraculously showed that Udar showed no trace of cancer. He can only attribute his wondrous cure to Amma's grace.

Amma in the mood of the Goddess Devi

In retrospect, he felt that the entire ordeal was the best thing to ever happen to him. He felt that the Goddess Devi gave him a trial by fire. For the first time in his life he felt completely helpless and humble. He stood before God completely naked, with his ego shattered. He felt that by facing death, he was able to bring his full attention and whole being to the altar of the present moment.

Udar told me that he finally understood what Ramakrisna Paramahansa (a saint from India who lived in the 19th century) meant when he said that a person should seek union with God like a man who runs to a lake because his hair is on fire. Udar feels that the ego-shattering experience has created an opening for Amma's grace to enter and help the lotus flower of his heart blossom.

An example of how Mother responds to our sincere prayers is illustrated in the story of Denise and Paul who have been devotees of Mother for many years. They had both been computer programmers who commuted from the East Bay to their jobs in the Silicon Valley. Unfortunately, Paul's health severely deteriorated a few years ago to the point where he has been unable to work. He became frustrated that Mother didn't help relieve his physical suffering and one day in 1994 when Mother was in San Ramon, he got so frustrated with the poor state of his health that he told his wife that he didn't even want any pictures of Mother in their house.

It was Mother's last day in San Ramon and Denise was very upset that her husband had become so cut off and angry with Amma. She silently cried and prayed to Mother for help incessantly throughout the day and even during the entire Devi Bhava that night. At the end of Devi Bhava when she went up for darshan, Denise was absolutely shocked when Mother spontaneously told her that she would come to their house.

That morning she asked several of the swamis when Mother would make the home visit. To her dismay, they all responded that Amma would be too busy to visit her house. Denise felt dejected since Mother was leaving San Ramon the following day. During the last evening's program in San Ramon, Denise asked Mother when she would come to her house, but Denise was heartbroken when Mother didn't answer the question.

Denise was aware that Mother has hundreds of requests from local devotees pleading with her to visit their house and felt that the visit was probably not going to happen. Amma's plane was scheduled to leave at 2:30 P.M. and as Denise paced in front of her house with a flickering light of hope in her heart, she realized that it was already 1:00 P.M. Paul shouted to his wife from inside the house, "I told you there is no way Mother is going to show up at our house."

He added, "She'll never come to someone's house who's angry at her when she could visit the hundreds of other houses full of devotees who love her."

Just as Paul finished his tirade, Denise noticed a blue van containing a very special passenger pull up into her driveway. Mother not only made a house visit, but she spent virtually the entire time talking to Paul. Mother's visit gave Denise the strength to deal with her husband's illness and helped Paul release his anger toward Mother for not healing him.

Mother's omniscience protects her devotees from danger as illustrated in the following stories. In India, a woman once left Devi Bhava in Amritapuri very late at night with her young son in order to catch a bus back to her little village. She realized that her son mistakenly had just gotten off the bus, so she quickly alighted from the coach at the next stop. It was very dark as she hurriedly walked back down the dusty road when, abruptly, a gang of tough-looking men surrounded her. Just when it looked as if they were ready to attack her, she cried out to Amma, "Oh Mother, I just came from Devi Bhava. Is this how you protect your daughter?"

Unexpectedly her eyes and tongue began to bulge out as her form grew larger and larger. The woman assumed the appearance of the fierce goddess Kali. The frightened ruffians immediately ran away.

During the July 2001 program in New York City, a female devotee was walking home alone after leaving the evening program. As the woman walked down a dimly lit side street, suddenly a man appeared out of nowhere and put a knife to her throat ordering her to give him all her money. The frightened woman, who was still filled with Amma's divine love, prayed to Mother for help. All of a sudden, the robber threw down his knife and said that he was sorry, that he didn't know why he tried to rob her. He ran away remorsefully.

Further evidence of Amma's omniscience occurred during July 2001 when a teenage boy, whose parents were ardent devotees of Amma, was involved in a very bad car accident. The young man was not driving carefully when his car skidded into a hillside demolishing the car. As the young man lay injured in his car, he suddenly had a vision of Mother standing in front of the windshield. She pointed to the left where he saw his dead body lying on the ground. It seemed she was indicating that this is what could have happened to him. She then told him to drive more carefully and disappeared. Since this traumatic, yet spiritually uplifting experience, the young man has become an enthusiastic devotee of Amma as well as a cautious driver.

Amma remembers every one of the millions of people who have seen her. On one occasion, a devotee was told that she could get darshan that day only if she was seeing Amma for the first time, since the darshan line was closed due to huge crowds. When she went up for darshan, Mother told one of the swamis that the woman had seen Mother before. The lady vehemently denied ever meeting Amma. However, when Amma again mentioned that the woman had met Mother, the woman finally sheepishly admitted that she really did see Amma previously but she never received an official darshan.

A friend of mine received darshan just once from Amma in 1991. Five years later he and his wife were travelling in India and visited Amritapuri, Mother's ashram in India. When they came up for darshan, Amma told my friend, "I remember you, but I never met your wife."

Mother is aware of all the activities that are simultaneously happening in the darshan hall. During the U.S. tour, Mother frequently speaks in Malayalam to the Indian devotees sitting nearby while giving darshan. This leaves Western disciples at quite a disadvantage. However, during the last morning of the retreat in Seattle a few years ago, I sat next to a Malayalam-speaking man who translated Amma's words. Amma told one of the swamis, "Some people got into the question line who shouldn't be there, but let them stay in line to ask their question or they will have to suffer another year waiting for an answer."

She then added, "The two people standing next to the pillar in the back of the hall are not part of the retreat. Tell them in a loving and kind manner to come back later for Devi Bhava."

The tour staff works for many long hours when Mother is in San Ramon during a two-week period, as well as maintaining a grueling schedule traveling to ten cities in six weeks. Some devotees work so many hours that they virtually never see Amma. Once, I told Amma that I felt badly when I would see some devotees sitting in front of her all the time as well as receiving darshan daily. I admitted that I was jealous since I didn't get to spend much time with Mother. She responded, "Mother is aware of everyone who is doing seva and is blessing them all the time."

She implied that the blessings that she showered on the *sevites* (devotees performing selfless service) were as powerful, if not stronger, than those devotees whom she was physically blessing. For instance, I have worked with a man named Cory who puts so much time and energy during Amma tours helping the pre-teen boys program that he rarely gets a chance to go to the hall to see Amma. In addition, after he finishes his work with the children, he frequently helps arrange shuttle rides for devotees.

During the retreats Mother serves dinner to all of the hundreds of participants. When Cory approached Amma to receive his plate, she stopped him and said, "Wait, here's a special large plate for you with lots of rice."

Mother was subtly acknowledging how selflessly he had performed seva. Amma gives the devotees extra energy so that they will be able to complete their seva. Many devotees have a selfless attitude toward seva and they feel that it is an honor just to be able to serve Amma, an incarnation of the Divine Mother.

Many hundreds of devotees are involved in performances for Amma every year throughout the world. One year a boy in the group of children I was supervising was in a skit that was performed for Amma. He was one of many boys involved in a short dance scene. The following year, the boys just sang bhajans for Amma. However, when the boy went up to receive darshan after the singing, Mother asked him, "Why didn't you dance this year like last year? Mother really enjoyed your dancing."

In a less dramatic illustration of Mother's omnipresent ability to help her children, during the 1999 summer tour I was very upset with another devotee a few hours before I went for darshan during Devi Bhava. Since I was very depressed when I lay my head on Mother's shoulder, she pulled me back and gazed deeply into my downcast eyes and asked, "Dayalu's sad?" I noticed that she said it loudly as she turned to her far right in the direction of the person with whom I was upset so the devotee would hear her. She then asked me to sit right down in front of her till the end of the program.

Mother can speak and understand all languages

Mother can tune her omnipresent consciousness anywhere she wants, since the entire universe is within her. She has the ability to speak different languages if she chooses. A woman from Yugoslavia came to India to see Amma several years ago. She was devastated emotionally since she had lost her husband and parents during her country's recent civil war. She told one of the swamis that due to the language barrier, she was afraid that Amma wouldn't understand her.

When the woman went up for her first darshan, Amma began gently singing to her, and suddenly the new devotee burst into tears. Later, the woman told a swami that Amma sang an old Yugoslavian folk song that she had not heard since her childhood when her own mother would sing it to her! The words of the song were, "Be happy, the world is as insubstantial as a dream, so don't let life make you sad." The elated woman returned to her homeland a few weeks later saturated with Amma's peace.

When people ask Mother questions in English she appears to need a translator to understand the devotees. However, Amma can understand everything if she so wishes. During the Seattle tour in 2001, I was asked to make an announcement concerning the magazine about Amma, "Immortal Bliss." Over the years I had made this announcement many times, so I wasn't particularly nervous when I recommended that the devotees subscribe to the magazine. I remembered that on the last day of a program in a tour city, it helps to emphasize that the local devotees can feel Mother's presence after she leaves their area by subscribing to the magazine.

I cleared my voice as I attempted to speak slowly and succinctly into the microphone, "Today is Mother's last day in Seattle and we are all sad." Before I could even finish the sentence, Mother yelled out, "This is not Mother's last day in Seattle and her children are not sad."

For someone who is supposed to need an interpreter, I was rather startled by the instant comeback. Everyone in the hall immediately began laughing.

All I could utter in response was, "This is not Mother's last day in Seattle (since she's omnipresent, she is always in the devotees' hearts) and her children are not sad but happy...but, if Mother's children want to be even happier they will subscribe to "Immortal Bliss."

At the beginning of the U.S. tour in 2001, the M.A. Center residents had an opportunity to meet with Mother in Seattle. One ashramite walked into the local devotee's house late and Amma asked him, "What is your name?"

He responded, "Adam."

Mother appeared to repeat the name a few times with difficulty saying, "Attam, Addum."

The devotee replied, "You can call me anything. Adam means from the Earth." Then he humbly added, "My name means mud."

Mother quickly responded, "A lotus blooms from the mud."

Adam had been bitten by many mosquitoes when he was in India and finally one day in frustration, he yelled, "I curse all the mosquitoes in Kerala."

Unfortunately, after he cursed the mosquitoes, he found that they would subsequently swarm all over him while ignoring everyone else and he frequently found himself bitten from head to toe. Finally, he went to Amma during a darshan in India and told her that mosquitoes were attacking him. He didn't tell her that he actually cursed the mosquitoes, but told her that he wanted to make peace with the insects and asked if she would help. She let out a hearty laugh, but said she would make a *sankalpa* (a resolve). She also told the interpreter that the question was very special and asked that the note with Adam's question be brought to her room.

When he was visiting India two years later, to his consternation, the mosquitoes were still fiercely biting Adam, causing him a great deal of physical pain. He finally cried to Amma from the depths of his heart to help him. Suddenly, the mosquitoes stopped biting him. They immediately flew away and never came back.

In Seattle in 2001 Amma told the small gathering of devotees that Adam cursed the mosquitoes and began laughing. He now prays for the well being of mosquitoes and even put them on the healing *archana* list (recitation of the names of Divine Mother dedicated to a healing).

In Boston Adam again arrived late to a meeting when the ashram residents were meeting with Amma. She chuckled when she saw him enter and shouted in perfect English, "You big dork!"

He responded, "Who me?"

Mother laughed, "Yes you, you big dork." Evidently, the perfect master can understand and speak even humorous slang in any language anytime she wants to.

MOTHER'S SUBTLE WAY OF HELPING HER CHILDREN

Although sometimes it's difficult to understand Amma's actions, everything she does is solely to help the devotees' spiritual development. During a satsang with ashram residents, Mother remarked, "Usually the guru will not tell things directly. It will be pointed out to you indirectly."

Ramakrishna Swami told a story of how he was travelling in a van with Amma, when all of the sudden she smacked him on his face. He was quite startled and didn't understand why his beloved Mother would hit him. Later she told him that he was destined at that moment to have a facial accident and by striking him, Amma mollified the effects of a potentially serious calamity.

I never understood why Mother so frequently asks a devotee, Chaitanya, to put blocks under her chair while she's giving darshan during the US tour. He has to awkwardly lift one side of the chair while Amma is sitting in it blessing people. One time when he picked up the chair, Amma suddenly yelled in Malayalam as if she was shocked that someone was moving her. She looked at Chaitanya and he suddenly experienced a bolt of love coming from her eyes which put him into quite a blissful state. He later told me that his most spiritually uplifting experiences have occurred when Mother has asked him to raise the chair, but then changes her mind and has him sit next to her.

At the end of one morning program when Mother was leaving the hall, I was preoccupied, feeling sorry for myself thinking that she never gives me attention. I was kneeling in a long row of devotees as she walked by when all of the sudden, smack, she bumped right into my shoulder. Mother then touched me and put her hand on her heart in the Indian gesture of apology. While at first I felt terrible that I thought I caused Mother to hurt herself, I realized later that she was subtly giving me the attention I craved.

For some strange reason during one year, I found myself spontaneously and frequently repeating out loud the word "*Shiva*" (The Hindu God of transformation), whether I was alone or with other people. I tried to control these Shiva outbursts when I was in public. However, once during a business meeting when I was working as a rehabilitation counselor, I spontaneously yelled "Shiva." When my colleagues gave me some rather strange looks, I quickly responded that we "should vie" to give the client the best rehabilitation program.

Shiva is the Hindu Deity who is the destroyer of the ego, allowing the devotee to merge into God's love. Amma and her disciples greet each other with the mantra "Om Namah Shivayah" which means I bow to God within you. That summer I asked Mother why I was incessantly repeating the name "Shiva" and she turned to me with a surprised look on her face and responded with a mischievous smile, "It's a good sign that you are saying Shiva."

Shiva

Mother played her part in this *leela* (divine play) impeccably as she acted astonished when I told what happened. However, I felt that she was really the one who subtly planted the deity's name in my consciousness.

MOTHER, THE OMNISCIENT JUDGE

From 1988 till 1995 I worked as a vocational rehabilitation counselor with a man who performed job development and labor market surveys for my clients. We talked to each other virtually everyday and occasionally I would meet with him at his home office where he lived with his attractive, soft-spoken wife and their four children aged five to fifteen. Jack, a tall, heavy-set man with thinning red hair, was a very pleasant person, who enjoyed making jokes and helping people. He would frequently take his family on weekend vacations and was very involved in his children's lives.

A few weeks after I moved into the ashram he called me up one afternoon to ask for my advice. He told me that his wife was having an affair with another man and that she wanted a divorce. I spent about thirty minutes listening to him and gave him some practical suggestions. I advised him to move out of the house as soon as possible due to the extreme tension between him and his wife, as well as to retain an attorney since he was concerned about losing his children, home and possessions. The following morning I was driving into San Ramon to do some errands when I heard a news bulletin about a shooting. As I began to change stations not wanting to hear about the latest local murder, I was horrified to hear that my colleague, Jack, was arrested for murdering his wife the previous afternoon. My entire body became numb with shock.

The following week I received a heart-wrenching letter from Jack telling me that his wife became angry with him and tried to shoot him. When he tried to grab the gun away from her, it accidentally went off, killing his wife. He then immediately called the police and tearfully related to me how his children came home from school to find their mother lying dead on the floor as the police were taking him handcuffed to jail.

Over the next few months Jack sent me many long and melancholy letters about his horrific situation. I remembered that he had virtually no friends (since his life revolved around his family), which is probably why he called me for help a few hours before the shooting. He expressed a great deal of concern about the fate of his children. I felt that it was dharmic for me to help him so I sent him supportive, uplifting letters as well as spiritual books that were written for prisoners.

When Mother arrived in the United States a few months later, I told her about my friend who was in jail accused of murdering his wife. Amma was shocked when I told her what had happened and asked me many questions about the case. I told her that the death was an accident and that Jack was a kind person as well as being a very caring father. She told me to support Jack in any way that I could.

I was asked to testify at the murder trial since I talked to Jack right before the incident. In his letters, Jack would constantly complain that his attorney never contacted him regarding evidence that he assembled that could prove his innocence. I called his attorney several times and the lawyer, whom I felt was incompetent, never returned my calls, nor asked to meet with me prior to my court appearance. However, the prosecuting attorney requested that I meet with him before I testified.

When I was being questioned under oath, I was impressed with the brilliant examination and questions that the prosecuting attorney asked me and was disappointed that the defense attorney hardly asked me anything although Jack constantly passed him notes. I felt that I could have prepared a better defense for Jack myself. During the course of the trial, I received several letters from Jack indicating that he wanted to fire his attorney because the lawyer was so inept in defending him.

A few weeks after my court appearance, I received a somber and heart-wrenching letter from Jack stating that he was sentenced to twenty years in prison for second degree murder. I felt that the American justice system was a sham, in as much as my friend received a twenty year prison sentence for a crime that I believed was an accident.

I asked Amma a few months after Jack was sent to the state penitentiary how I could help my pitiable friend. I explained to Mother that he didn't receive a fair trial due to his incompetent attorney. I had supported him for the last year, testified on his behalf and believed that he shot his wife in self-defense. Mother's response really surprised me. "He committed the murder, don't contact him. He'll put his burden on you."

I had really wanted to help my friend whom I believed to be innocent, yet Mother's advice prevented me from falling into a murderer's web of deceit. I later contemplated how the beleaguered criminal justice system could be reformed if someone of Mother's stature was a judge and felt so grateful that I am a disciple of an omniscient being such as Amma.

In another case, there was a American teenage boy whose parents were ardent devotees of Amma. Evan, a tall, thin seventeen year old boy who wore his long brown hair in a pony tail, had received many loving darshans from Amma over the last eight years, but as an adolescent he wasn't interested in going for darshan when Amma visited New York City. During the New York programs, his parents told Amma that they were concerned about their son, who had begun hanging out with a bunch of drug-using boys and who had recently been arrested for selling drugs himself.

A week after Amma left Manhattan, Evan and three other teenage boys were arrested for burglary. Evan's attorney told him while he was being held in jail without bail that it looked like he would be sent to Youth Authority for at least one year since he already had a prior offense on his record. When the attorney left his jail cell, Evan began crying and praying deeply for help. Suddenly Mother's form materialized in front of him in the juvenile hall cell and she told him, "I will save you this time, but if you get in trouble again you will have to suffer the consequences of your actions."

Miraculously, Evan's case was dismissed on a technicality. The vision of Amma changed his life and consequently he stopped using drugs and is now attending college.

Mother's grace creates a program site

I was asked to try to find a suitable location for Mother's November, 2000 tour in the Bay Area. We were unable to hold programs at the ashram that year because of problems having to do with county regulations. I spent many hours contacting various facilities, but to my dismay I found out that most large convention centers and hotels were reserved at least a year in advance. Unfortunately, I was contacting facilities in August for the November program. After hundreds of phone calls, I finally found one center in Oakland that had an opening the week Mother would be in the Bay Area. I became quite proud of myself as I fantasized that "I" had found the perfect site, therefore, Amma would give me special attention for assuring Mother's visit to the Bay Area.

However, as my mind began creating various scenarios of adulation for the great work I accomplished, I suddenly became worried. I thought to myself, "What if Amma doesn't like the site or what if something terrible happened at the center, since it was near an unsafe neighborhood? It would be all my fault."

I told Dayamrita Swami that maybe we shouldn't have the program in Oakland because I didn't want to be responsible if anything went wrong.

He replied, "You think what happens actually has anything to do with you? What takes place is all in Mother's hands."

I felt somewhat relieved upon hearing his response and could then safely revert to my egotistical fantasies of how I saved the day for the Divine Mother just like the monkey god Hanuman helped Ram by saving Sita in the Indian scripture Ramayana. I arranged a meeting with the director of the Oakland center and felt quite self- important as I coordinated the meeting, which included three swamis and a board member.

However, instead of vanquishing the demon Ravana in Lanka and saving Sita, I let the demon ego within destroy my spiritual progress. Consequently, a few weeks after my presumed victory for Amma, I was told by the director of the Oakland facility that they were canceling our program since the group that had already signed a contract didn't want to share the building. It was now sixty days before Mother's scheduled visit to the Bay Area and I felt like I should be exiled from the ashram for ruining Mother's chances of having a program in the Bay Area. Instead of the monkey god Hanuman saving the day, the baboon Dayalu ruined the day.

I humbly prayed deeply to Amma the next morning during meditation to help me locate a program site so that the devotees would be able to experience Amma's bliss in November. That morning I mentioned to an ashram resident that I had called every possible hall in the Bay Area and every place was booked. The devotee asked me if I called Marin Civic Center and, with my know-it-all attitude, I responded that I'm sure that they wouldn't have any space available, even though that was the one possible hall that I failed to contact. Just to satisfy the devotee's inquiry, I made a pointless phone call to the Marin Center and no one returned my call for days.

However, the following week I received a call from the director of the Marin Center who told me that the week that I wanted the hall just happened to be the only opening that they had available all year! I told her that our organization was very interested in renting their facility, but that I would have to discuss the details with other members of our organization.

The next morning, Friday, I received another call from the director of the Marin Center informing me that the group that usually books their center for that week in November just called and wanted to make a reservation. I was informed that we needed to give them a deposit immediately or we would lose the space.

Remembering that Ammachi was flying to New York City the following day to give a talk at the 50th anniversary of the United Nations, I told the Marin Center director that our CEO will be in town this weekend and asked if I could let her know our decision on Monday. Amma told the board of directors to have all the programs at the Marin Center and we ended up reserving the facility immediately. This extraordinary turn of events helped me realize how everything is in the hands of the Holy Mother and her divine flow manifests only when I get my ego out of the way.

CHAPTER II

Amma's lessons for the disciple

"It is not possible to get close to God if there is no sorrow of some kind. Therefore, God will create some kind of difficulties through Mother. Having heated the iron in the fire, the blacksmith beats it. It is not possible to beat it into a shape without heating it up properly.

"The guru will create obstacles and sorrows for the disciple. The disciple should overcome all that with intense sadhana. Spiritual practice is not for idle people. The difficulties of the subtle level are hard compared to the sorrows of the external world. However, there is nothing to fear for one who dedicates everything to a Satguru."

THE IMPORTANCE OF DISCRIMINATION

One evening as I was about to grab a quick dinner before beginning my seva with the pre-teen boys. Rasya, who worked in the bookstore, told me there was a truck arriving full of books and there was no one to unload the truck. I really wanted to eat my dinner, but I felt that I should help. I over-reacted and began asking others if they could help. I figured that with more devotees unloading the truck, the job would be finished sooner and I could quickly return to the important task of devouring my delicious dinner.

In a matter of minutes, I ran down to the white barn, with ten people I had found, to help me unload the truck. When we arrived, Rasya said that she didn't need our help since there was only one pallet and she already had two devotees unloading the books. In retrospect, if I had calmly walked over to the truck and found out how many books were needed to be unloaded, I wouldn't have ended up disturbing ten people's lives as well as my own.

During a satsang with Amma, I told her that sometimes I get upset with God. The omnipotent Creator gave humans free will and we keep making mistakes with this ability. I remarked that I felt hopeless that I couldn't free myself from the karma that I've created in previous births since the negative tendencies I have only result in my creating more bad karma for myself in this incarnation.

Mother responded, "You are not going to gain anything by being upset with God; just try to correct your own mistakes. We should use the proper discrimination to help others and understand that whatever has happened is in the past and not to brood over it. Try to change yourself through your discrimination rather than trying to change others."

Lessons in detachment

In November 1997 I had the opportunity of being the tour parking coordinator at the M.A. Center in San Ramon. Some of the challenges of helping to park cars include the opportunity to stand outside in mud during freezing, bone-chilling November rainstorms for hours on end; or to sweat under the hot, June sun inhaling dust as cars speed by. The parking lot attendant has to inform harried and late arrivals driving into the ashram with less than four passengers that they have to drive to the carpool lot five miles away.

While most devotees are cooperative, I'll always have fond memories of certain drivers, like the haughty lady wearing a fur coat and high heels who drove into the ashram in her new, red jaguar demanding to park on the road in front of the temple. When she was told that she couldn't park there, she responded, "Go ahead and give me a ticket if you don't like it."

Then there was the famous Hollywood movie star who drove up in a chauffeur driven limo, and insisted on parking right in front of the temple, completely blocking access for Mother's car to pick her up at the end of the program.

I also affectionately remember the delightful individual who parked his car in the middle of the road so Mother's car couldn't get by. When I finally found the man eating in the dining room and asked him to please move his car, he responded in a loud, abrasive voice, "Hey why don't ya chill out. Can't ya see I'm busy eating now. Don't worry, I'll get to it later."

During the November 1997 tour, some cars had entered two of the parking lots early in the morning before the staff was on duty and parked in such a way that limited the number of cars that were able to be parked. Since we were expecting a huge influx of vehicles for Devi Bhava that night, I made several announcements asking people to please move their cars. However, the devotees did not want to leave Mother to go out into the cold to move their cars. Finally, I asked Amma what to do and she told me emphatically, "Tell them that their cars will be towed away if they don't move them now."

As soon as I mentioned that cars would be towed away, many people went running out of the temple to move their cars. However, several people became infuriated. One man screamed at me, full of ire, "How dare you threaten to tow my car away. You control-freaks made me lose my place in the darshan line. Who is your boss? I want to know what idiot approved such a stupid announcement. I'd like to give your supervisor a piece of my mind."

I remained quiet but was very tempted to tell him, "See that little lady up front with the white sari hugging people. You may want to give her a piece of your mind." Although I remained silent, I was fuming inside due to my inability to be detached.

I usually coordinate the distribution of the holy water during the Devi Puja. After I completed this seva assignment one year, a swami asked me to make sure that the little children and babies were quiet, especially during the meditation. During the puja, parents with little children and infants can watch the ceremony on the large closed-circuit television in the dining structure where the babies wouldn't disturb the ceremony.

During the puja a baby nearby began crying loudly, so I asked the mother in a very gentle manner if she could please take the baby outside so it wouldn't disturb people who are meditating. The woman very indignantly responded that it was too cold outside, but then proceeded to walk out of the hall. However, she returned with the howling infant a few minutes later. After the puja I went up to the woman and told her that I felt badly that I had to ask her to leave. She tersely responded, "Don't you know that the sound of a crying baby is the sound of God?"

When I told her that a swami asked me to make sure it was quiet during the puja, she began shouting "A swami or Mother would never ask a baby to leave the hall. How dare you lie to me." I walked away feeling enraged with the inconsiderate woman.

Since I feel that I really didn't get the lesson of detachment, Amma arranged a similar incident for me the following day. My seva assignment that year was to coordinate the pre-teen boys program. The young lads tend to run around in little groups sometimes creating a bit of a ruckus. During the programs some of the more creative boys have engaged in various fun activities such as: putting peanut butter on door handles in hotels; throwing boxes of soap detergent in swimming pools; breaking water pipes by jumping off tree limbs; and the ubiquitous target practice of throwing rocks at all sorts of animate and inanimate objects.

We started a program for the boys to direct their exuberant energy into a positive spiritual direction. However, one day during the summer tour in San Ramon, I saw a boy mischievously and methodically knocking all the leaves off one of our apple trees with a big stick. I then observed his mother standing near him. I introduced myself to the mother and told her about the special pre-teen boys program. I also told her that we have a rule at the M.A. Center that children need to be with

The annual children's retreat at the M.A. Center with Dayamrita Swami

their parents or in one of the childcare programs. She became extremely upset and told me that her son was nine years old and much too old to be told what to do.

Actually her son was basically a very good boy, but just needed some direction. Throughout the two weeks of Mother's visit in San Ramon, I kept trying to help the free-spirited mother create structure for her son, trying to come from a place of compassion and detachment. Although she became angry with me a few more times, I tried not to be reactive with her. Finally, on the last day of the San Ramon program, she very responsibly came to check her son into the children's program and I subsequently thanked her for all her help. She then broke down crying, telling me that she was experiencing a lot of sadness and anger the last few weeks. My heart went out to her as I empathized with her pain while she was being purified in the presence of Amma.

Patience will lead one to the goal

Recently I had to call my health insurance company since my policy was being changed. I found myself getting increasingly frustrated wasting so much time pressing different buttons to get through to a human being on the automated phone system. "Press one for English. Press two if you have a current policy. Enter your policy number. Press three to learn about new health benefits...that is not a valid entry; press four to return to the main menu... you have pressed an invalid entry two times so you are now being disconnected!" When I called back on the fourth attempt, I actually pressed the right set of numbers and I was finally on deck to talk to a human being. I was then informed that my waiting time was only fifteen minutes.

When I finally talked to an actual person, I was fuming as I told the poor operator what an inefficient and incompetent company she worked for. So much for exhibiting the quality of patience that Amma tells the devotees we must develop in order to grow spiritually. However, after I finished my tirade, a lady with a very centered, soft-spoken voice exhibiting a slight accent apologized for the long wait.

I told her that she had a very calming voice and a soothing accent, so I asked her where she was from. She responded that she was from Bombay, India. I then proceeded to tell her that my guru was from India. However, I was embarrassed to tell the insurance employee that I was a disciple of Ammachi since I had behaved so rudely at the beginning of the conversation. I didn't want her to know that such an impatient, discourteous person was associated with Amma.

However, when I finally mentioned Amma's name, she became very excited and told me that she met Amma ten years ago and that she had Mother's picture on her altar. She then told me that although she saw Amma just one time, that very morning she was wondering how she could see her again and felt despondent since she had no information when Amma would be in Los Angeles. After giving her the schedule of Amma's next program in her area and telling her stories about Mother, I felt exhilarated by the synchronicity of events. The next time I have to wrestle with an automated phone system, hopefully I will be more patient remembering that the long wait could be a harbinger for a deep spiritual connection.

Obedience to the guru

In 1996 a group of men living in the ashram started playing volleyball on Sunday mornings. Ron, who now lives in India directing Mother's AIMS hospital, mentioned to Swami Amritaswarupananda, whom we affectionately call "Big Swamiji," that some of the men in the California ashram were playing volleyball. When Swamiji heard the news, he became excited exclaiming, "Volleyball was my favorite game in college. I'd like to play sometime when I'm in San Ramon."

Swamiji and Amma arriving at the temple in San Ramon

I asked Swamiji if we should put up the volleyball net when he was staying in San Ramon during the winter of 2000, but he wanted to ask Amma for her permission when he met her in Australia. Amma gave her approval for Swamiji to play.

Big Swamiji has a rather forceful and dynamic energy, to say the least, so he magnetized the devotees to the volleyball court and we all had a great time playing everyday. Nevertheless, after several weeks of daily diving for the volleyball, jumping up and down and smashing the ball, many of the devotees began sustaining injuries. I hurt my knee and other people including Swamiji developed orthopedic injuries. I told Swamiji that when Amma arrives this summer, she will be able to tell who the volleyball players are because when we bow down to her, we won't be able to get up off the floor. In spite of the injuries, we all had a lot of fun and looked forward to playing when Swamiji returned to San Ramon the following year.

The following Spring, in anticipation of more vedic volleyball victories, I prepared the court by pulling out weeds and grading the court with the tractor. However, when Swamiji arrived in San Ramon, he told me that Mother felt it was best that he didn't play volleyball due to his role in a traditional Hindu ashram. Naturally he obeyed Amma and even though the residents missed the exciting games, we understood that following the guru's game plan will lead us to the eternal, divine court.

In an attempt to save money so that more donations could go directly to helping the poor, Mother decided in November 2001 to reduce the childcare staff. The pre-teen boys program staff was cut from three to just myself. I was told that Mother wanted volunteers to supervise the program. During the previous summer tour, I tried to recruit volunteers for the program, but after asking at the seva desk daily, not one devotee volunteered. Even though I was able to recruit one full time volunteer for November, I believed that the childcare program would fail since one volunteer and myself couldn't supervise up to twenty-five boys at least eight hours a day.

Rather than obeying Amma's instructions, I foolishly told Mother that no one ever volunteers for the boys program and the program can't function without more adult staff. She responded curtly that I should keep asking at the seva desk for help. I felt it was worthless obeying Mother, but I begrudgingly sauntered over to the seva desk and mentioned to the seva co-ordinator to keep asking the devotees if they could help with the childcare program. A man overheard my request and said he would be glad to volunteer. As a matter of fact, between the parents and many new volunteers, the program was more successful than ever. I had forgotten that when Mother makes a sankalpa we need to unequivocally obey her, since with her grace anything is possible.

Mother loves change

In the summer of 2001 I arrived at Mother's house in San Ramon an hour before she was scheduled to arrive from Seattle. The devotees were scurrying around making last minute changes preparing for the Divine Mother's imminent arrival. One of the devotees wanted to know if we should bring food from the main house located a half mile away in case Mother wanted to serve something to the devotees when she arrived. Big Swamiji was called on his cell phone as he and Amma were driving toward the M.A. Center from the airport. The response was clear: Amma was not going to serve food to anyone.

However, as soon as Mother walked in the door, she wanted to serve lunch to all the devotees. Pradeep (a normally calm and easy-going young man from India) and I quickly jumped into his clean, blue car and sped to the main house. I thought Amma just wanted to give *prasad* (sacred offering, usually food), so I put some of the Indian delicacies that were simmering in huge pots on the stove into a few large containers while Pradeep decided to grab some of the gigantic vessels of Indian food.

Knowing Mother was waiting for the food, we hurriedly loaded the containers and pots into the car. As we sped down the curvy hill and over the pot-holed, dirt road, much of the soup and legumes splattered all over the car and us. As we carried the half-empty, messy-looking pots toward Mother who was waiting in the kitchen to serve the sumptuous repast, Pradeep and I tried wiping off the streams of curry and yogurt that were flowing down our white clothes. Mother laughed exuberantly as she observed the *shraddha* (awareness) of her slovenly sons. After examining the pathetic state of the containers of Indian delicacies, she asked, "What, no rice?," at which point the Olympic food race commenced anew. In retrospect, I understand that every act of the guru helps us to release old *vasanas* (latent ego tendencies) and develop concentration and awareness. Who can estimate how much karma Mother is burning up for her children by constantly making changes?

At the commencement of Devi Bhava in Seattle in 2001, Mother mentioned that the floor on the stage was too low and

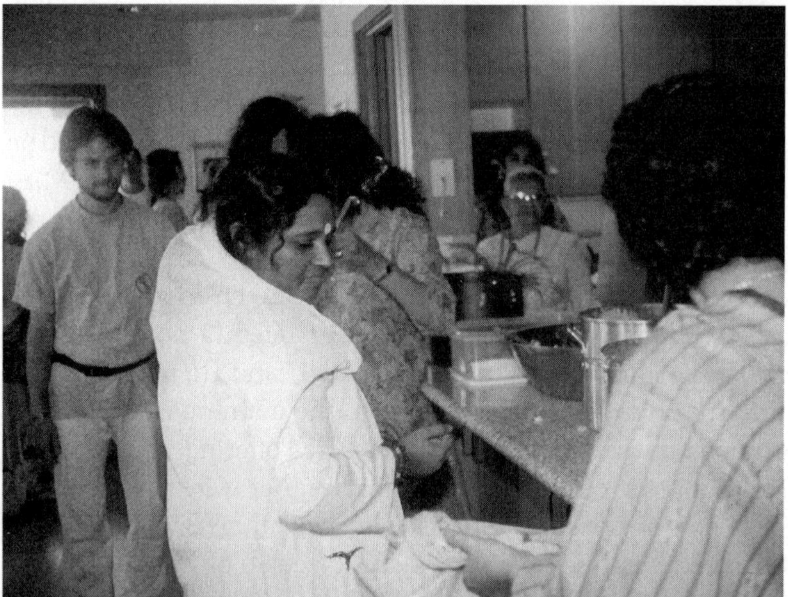

Mother prepares to serve food to her children in San Ramon

she requested a cushion for the devotees to kneel on when they approached her for darshan. Quickly Ramakrishna Swami, Chaitanya and I began taping together some foam, but it appeared too slippery to kneel on. Then we obtained some rugs and began taping them together. The entire project looked rather dubious. However, Ramakrishna Swami was insistent that we create a temporary riser since Mother had asked for it. After much scurrying around, Ramakrishna Swami and I laboriously maneuvered the ugly, taped rug up toward Mother where we would have to stop the darshan line to put the monstrosity in front of Amma's chair. She looked at the work of art and exclaimed, "Put it to the side. Maybe I'll use it later." Ah, more karma being burnt up by the Divine Mother.

A few years ago when I was flying with Mother from Los Angeles to Albuquerque, I was looking forward to spending time in the Phoenix airport where we changed planes with just a few devotees and Amma. I relished the thought that there would be no one waiting at the Phoenix airport to greet Ammachi and that we would have the Holy Mother all to ourselves. As we descended into the Phoenix airport, I plotted how I could obtain the closest seat to her as we waited in the terminal for an hour between plane connections.

Like a running back in a championship football game, I huddled with myself on how to quickly get past my opponents, the passengers, and score a touchdown by beating the other devotees to Amma. As I adroitly maneuvered past the opposition, I knew that victory was at hand as I reached the goal line of the nearest seat to Amma. However, to my dismay, as I sat down next to Mother, she playfully interacted with all the other devotees in the waiting area, but totally ignored me as if I were confined to the third-string team.

The following year when the tour entourage had a stopover in Phoenix, I had no expectations of spending any time with Mother and withdrew from the ruthless and competitive game of "pushing your way to Amma." However, Mother suddenly decided to disembark from the plane and I had the good karma to spend about thirty minutes sitting with Mother and a few devotees. She talked in English about the meaning of *Shivaratri* (celebration of Lord Shiva) and handed us prasad. At one point she looked deeply into my eyes as I realized I had a huge grin on my face. After she gave me prasad, she looked at me and said "Dayalu, did you get prasad?" Mother changed the manner in which she treated me when I became more humble. Behaving in a more modest manner, there is an opening for Divine Mother's sweet energy to enter.

During the 1999 summer tour, Mother was experiencing some physical pain and the close devotees expressed a great deal of concern about her ability to continue giving darshan. When Mother arrived in the white van at her house for the retreat at Fort Flagler, an old army base outside of Seattle, I put my hand out so she could be supported in case she needed help going down the steps. I was shocked to experience her full weight leaning on me as she slowly and painfully extricated herself from the vehicle. I noticed that she was experiencing difficulty walking toward the two-story white clapboard house. I was very worried that after more than twenty years of people leaning on her small body, she would finally be unable to continue hugging millions of devotees all over the world.

Before the evening program began I decided to stand near the stage to help Mother up the five steps. I wondered how she could possibly ascend the stairs given the difficulty she appeared to experience earlier in the day just getting out of the van. As Amma entered the darshan hall it appeared that every cell of her body was radiating joy and bliss, which was in such stark contrast from the pain-ridden body she exhibited a few hours earlier. She smiled toward all the devotees as she moved swiftly toward the stage. I put my hand out as she approached the steps, but she waved me away as she bounded up the stairs full of vim and vigor.

I pondered many theories of why she suddenly didn't need help going up the stairs. Maybe she really didn't need help getting out of the van but was just answering my prayer. I incessantly repeated for weeks before Mother arrived in the United States, "Amma please take my hand and lead me to the other shore."

Maybe she does experience physical pain but when she wants to, she's able to transcend body consciousness. I've seen her look quite pained and disheveled at the end of a darshan, only to see her exuberant, energetic and blissful a few hours later. However, my miniscule brain couldn't possibly comprehend the fathomless depth of the incarnation of the Divine Mother of the Universe.

Mother's many sacrifices for her children

I've been blessed to have the opportunity to perform the cherished *seva* (selfless service) known as lap seva. This job requires the sevite to make sure that people are put correctly on Amma's lap as Mother hugs each devotee in turn. This job is incredibly intense. Kneeling next to Amma and trying to make sure that no one inadvertently hurts her demands the utmost concentration. Performing seva under the direct observation of the Holy Mother for a sustained period of time can be quite an extraordinary experience.

An important aspect of the lap position is to make sure no one accidentally hurts Amma, while keeping the line running smoothly. Although the devotees coming up for darshan are asked not to grab Amma, occasionally people ecstatically grasp her body. I try to put everyone's hand on her chair as they come up for darshan, but it's not always physically possible- for example, when I'm simultaneously trying to help a disabled person getting up after darshan. However, if a devotee is already clutching Amma, Mother won't let me pull the person's hand away, even if the devotee is causing Amma pain.

Can you imagine what it must feel like to have thousands of people falling on you and grasping at you all day long every day of the year?

Mother sometimes keeps one foot sticking out of the cushion where she rests her feet. During one darshan, a very obese, handicapped woman hobbled up toward Amma leaning heavily on her cane. I told her that she didn't have to try to kneel, if that was too difficult for her. She indicated that she would stand while receiving her hug. At the last moment she fell on her knees landing on Mother's foot cushion. Thankfully, she just missed falling right on the lotus feet of our beloved Amma.

I have actually witnessed people push onto Mother's feet, yet Amma won't react to the severe pain for fear of emotionally upsetting the darling child who had just injured her. I've also observed people suddenly leaning on Amma's legs to get up after darshan instead of bracing themselves on the arms of the chair. Through all these painful experiences, Mother has never complained to the careless devotee.

Amma's mind is always thinking of how to spiritually help the devotees. Like a mother who misses her child, Amma is saddened if the devotees who want to spend time with her are financially unable to do so.

On one occasion, I was boarding an airplane with Amma at the Seattle airport. I ended up standing right behind Amma as we waited in line in the hallway just before entering the aircraft. There was a non-devotee in front, so Mother and I were standing alone for a few moments. She gazed at me with a sorrowful expression in her eyes and sadly whispered, "Problem, children have no money to fly to San Ramon."

She was referring to the many devotees who came to see Amma off at the airport who could not afford to go on the rest of the tour. I told her that maybe they could drive to California. She shook her head, indicating that was not a practical solution, and appeared very despondent. Mother's eyes then appeared to be traveling through various *lokas* (worlds) as if she were compassionately helping sentient and insentient beings throughout the Universe.

Mother's inspiration feeds the poor

Amma has inspired thousands of people all over the world to help uplift suffering humanity by alleviating the anguish of the poor. She has created the largest multi-purpose hospital in Cochin, India; developed hospices for the terminally ill; assumed responsibility for orphanages; created vocational training schools; and built hundreds of homes for the poor.

The Amrita Institute of Medical Sciences in Cochin, India

Amma has motivated hundreds of devotees in cities throughout the United States to feed the poor in a program called "Mother's Kitchen." Her inspiration motivated a small group of devotees residing in a very rural area in the Sierra Mountains of Northern California to serve the poor where I recently assisted in joyfully preparing a nutritious, vegetarian meal.

As I chopped vegetables, I reminisced about another time I was preparing a meal during a small retreat in San Ramon in 1991. I was mindlessly chopping chard, and chatting about inconsequential subjects such as the cost of housing and the commute time in the Bay Area, when Mother suddenly walked onto the deck of the main house. She unexpectedly came up to me and took the knife and vegetables out of my hand and proceeded to show me how to properly cut the greens. As she rolled the chard into an impeccable snake-like form, I beheld perfection with each chop of the knife. As Amma skillfully cut the greens, she repeated, "Mantra, mantra, mantra."

Remembering the lesson Mother taught me ten years earlier, I began chanting my mantra with each chop of the knife as I cut chard and kale. At that moment a devotee mentioned, "Mother's everywhere."

I thought of how the divine light of Ammachi has created sparks of love and compassion for the poor throughout the world: providing nourishing meals for an elderly, homeless woman in the ghetto of Chicago as well as for a toddler living in a shack at a migrant worker camp in California; offering an educational opportunity for a teenager living in the steaming slums of Bombay and also for an orphan in rural Kerela; subsidizing a life-saving surgery for an indigent girl from an impoverished village in Southern India and providing the same for a frail octogenarian from Madras. Amma's lamp of service to the poor is truly spreading love and sustenance throughout the world, alleviating the suffering of humanity.

Children in one of Amma's schools in India blessing their food

When Mother left San Ramon in June 2001 to continue on her US tour, there were only a few ashram residents who stayed behind. I noticed that there were a lot of perishable food items left in the walk-in refrigerator that the few remaining residents wouldn't be able to consume. Thinking of Mother's emphases of always helping the poor, I contacted a church in Oakland where members of the M.A. Center community have cooked for Mother's kitchen program.

The church kitchen manager was thrilled when I told her about all the food that I wanted to donate. However, my car was too small to transport the large containers of food and the remaining ashram trucks were not working. I was pondering how to transport all the food to the church while I was driving out of the ashram later that day. I suddenly remembered that a devotee named Thomas who lived in Oakland near the church owned a pickup truck. Just as I reached the end of the dirt road, to my surprise, I noticed Thomas driving into the ashram in his truck. I asked him if he could take the food to Oakland and he replied, "Sure, if you help me load the food I can do it now."

I immediately called the church director and fortuitously reached her although it was already after closing hours. By Amma's grace, food for the poor was immediately donated to the church kitchen.

Mother's practical advice regarding money

Before I studied vedic astrology, an astrologer predicted that in April of 1994 I would need to be careful regarding money since I was entering an inauspicious financial ten year cycle. For my entire adult life I never had a problem obtaining any job that I wanted or earning a good income. While I definitely have had challenging karma to deal with in many areas, I always believed I would be successful in my career so I didn't take the astrological advice seriously.

However, on the exact day that I began my difficult cycle, I invested my life savings in what appeared to be a very successful small business. Unexpectedly, the company went out of business two years later, resulting in a total loss of all my savings. Besides this huge financial loss, the California legislature made changes in the vocational rehabilitation system in 1994 whereby I would no longer be able to continue working in my successful career.

When I told Amma in 1997 that I lost my life savings, she surprisingly asked me, "Didn't you lose the money last year?"

It was reassuring to know that Ammachi, the one who sees all the actions of the disciples, was aware of my financial woes before I discussed them with her. I responded, "It looked like I lost the money last year, but it wasn't until this year that the loss became official."

She then began asking me many practical questions about the investment, such as, "Where did you invest the money?

How much did you lose? Why couldn't you have taken the money out sooner? What interest rate were you getting?"

I confessed to Mother that the real reason I invested my money in the now defunct business was greed, since I wanted the higher interest rate that they were offering.

Mother is very practical when it comes to money. Every grain of rice is important to her since she is always concerned about how to alleviate the suffering of the poor. Mother is always looking for ways of saving money whether it is keeping tour staff positions to a minimum, declining to have programs at luxurious facilities or asking many devotees to share one room. What is a little delay or inconvenience in comparison to giving a nourishing meal to a starving child or providing medical care that could save the life of a baby? In retrospect, if I had used more discrimination regarding my finances, I could have helped relieve the suffering of the poor rather than unsuccessfully trying to accumulate more wealth.

Mother is also extremely pragmatic when giving advice to devotees regarding career choices. She frequently recommends devotees to study in college and obtain a useful skill, rather than just running off to live in her ashram. Amma has also created many technical schools for the poor so that they will be able to earn a good living.

Since my former, successful career had totally disintegrated in 1994, I tried a new business venture of teaching stress reduction classes. When I asked her about pursuing this vocational goal, Amma indicated that my prospects in this field were not good. Later, I asked Amma, "Will working as a vedic astrologer be prosperous since Amma said Dayalu's stress reduction program wouldn't be successful?"

Mother understood the subtleties of my challenging career *prarabdha* (karma) and replied, "It's like a lottery, eventually something will click in if you keep trying."

Consequently, I have noticed that during challenging astrological periods, it's still important to put out energy and not give up hope. I believe that we always have free will as to how we deal with challenging karmic situations.

While finances have been a challenge for me since 1994, I noticed that in the Spring of 2001 some favorable astrological financial transits would occur. The day Mercury was transiting Rahu in my eleventh house of money, I received a huge unexpected check in the mail. A few days later when Jupiter was transiting Rahu, another large check arrived out of the blue.

My attitude as a yogi living in an ashram should be one of detachment. When I follow Amma's message of focusing on what is real (which is anything that can never be destroyed), it's easier to be detached from the illusory financial ups and downs of the Nasdaq waves. However, I think that I might need a little more practice in developing detachment. When I received the unexpected windfall, I joyfully danced and yelled, "All right, yes, yes, yes, I got money, I got money."

The innocence of a child

Mother has often told the devotees that it is beneficial for one's spiritual growth to have the innocence of a child. While at one moment Mother can be teaching the devotees the highest spiritual truths, at the next, she can instantaneously begin playing like a child. I've seen her totally enthralled, flying a kite or playing tag with little children while minutes later give an inspiring talk to thousands on the complexities of living a spiritual life.

For the last few years my seva when Amma is in San Ramon has been working with the pre-teen boys. While twenty pre-adolescent boys can create quite a disturbance at times, they are also overflowing with innocent, pure energy. While some people avoid this *seva* like the plague, Cory, Nirupama and myself have enjoyed this high energy job. When I follow Amma's advice of having the innocence of a child by enthusiastically playing with the children, I feel a spontaneous flow of positive energy and joy flowing through me.

Most pre-adolescent boys are not particularly interested in attending *bhajans* (devotional singing to God) or listening to adult spiritual talks. They would rather play games, eat snacks and act silly. However, Dayamrita Swami, myself and other adults have led spiritual discussions geared toward their level that the boys really enjoyed. In their innocence, I found the elementary school children receptive to certain spiritual concepts, such as the importance of helping people, rather than just always playing; sharing their games and toys; and a profound understanding of the law of karma.

Many years ago I worked in an alternative school where the children were free to do as they wished with virtually no rules. However, I now understand how important it is to create a struc-

Amma's little children coming for darshan

ture for children. Mother frequently discusses the importance of giving love to the very young children, while teaching spiritual values to the older children through structure. Last year during the San Ramon tour, the children would line up nightly to sing bhajans for Mother as her car would drive by on the way to the Temple. However, some children would try to run after the car, creating a potentially dangerous situation. Mother normally treats the little children very gently and with much tenderness, yet one night she rolled down the car window and sternly instructed, "Stay back from the car; it's very dangerous."

It required this stern admonishment from Mother to put an end to the children's innocent, yet potentially dangerous behavior.

Sometimes when we see a gang of wild-looking boys running around, playing aggressively or throwing rocks, it's easy to forget that underneath the macho bravado are sweet and vulnerable little children.

One of the boys in my pre-teen group sent me the following email before the summer 2001 tour:

> *Hi Dayalu,*
>
> *School is good and my favorite subject is math. I have a few personal questions I am wondering if I could ask you.*
>
> *I am wondering if you can tell me what's it like to die because I am kind of afraid.*
>
> *I am also wondering if I'll ever see my Grandma again. She passed away two years ago and when I think of her I get sad because I miss her and would like to see her.*
>
> *When I die can I be an angel with God up in heaven or come back as a little boy's guardian angel? Maybe*

I can be a guardian angel for a little boy like me who is also scared so that I can help him.

Is it ok to want something other than God; like wanting to be a famous football player or like going in a store and seeing something I like and is it O.K. to want it?

Your dear friend,

Daryl

I was touched by the sweetness and innocence of the letter and tried to respond in a way that Amma would want me to, so I feebly attempted to answer Daryl's poignant questions.

Dear Daryl,

I'm also afraid to die because I don't know exactly what it will be like. However, my dad died two months ago and I experienced in deep meditation that my dad seemed full of joy. I've talked to many people who have had similar experiences, sensing that their loved one is very happy. So even though it is scary to die, from everything I've experienced and heard from Amma and the great saints is that the soul will be happy when we leave the body. It's kind of like having an old car that doesn't run so well anymore, so we have to trade it in for a new model.

I also miss my dad, which is natural. While you may not be able to see your Grandma, she may still be able to watch over you and help you from the other side like a guardian angel. Amma says everyone who is with her in this life has been with her before so I believe we will "see" our loved ones again, but maybe in a different form. Amma told me that my dog that died was reborn as a girl so the form may change but the love won't die.

Maybe you'll be a guardian angel. The important thing is to be kind and loving to people now and then you will be a guardian angel on Earth for many other scared little boys.

Of course it's fine to want to be a famous football player or want something in a store. However, just remember that everything comes from God and to thank God for all his gifts that he's given you. Frequently, I've seen famous athletes thanking God for their talent. God wouldn't have created nice things in the store if He didn't want you to enjoy them. Enjoy everything, live in the present and don't worry, be happy. God loves you very much as does Amma, your family, friends and me.

Dayalu

Several ashram residents work as substitute teachers in the local school system since it gives us the opportunity to earn some income, yet to be available to be with Amma on tour. Working as a substitute teacher, I have found that children are open to learning spiritual principles when they are presented in an exciting format. When I teach school, I have noticed that the children who are having a difficult time understanding math or reading feel badly about themselves. I try to build the children's self-esteem by telling them that everyone is good at different things and being talented in one subject is not better than being proficient in another area. I then ask each child in the class what they enjoy doing and what they are good at. Sometimes I teach the children about karma surreptitiously by telling them stories of when I was in grade school. For example, I relate the story of how I tried to get away with not having my parents sign a note, only to be caught later at a parent-teacher conference.

I especially enjoy building up the self-esteem of the student in the class who has been labeled as the "bad" child. Since I was hyperactive in elementary school in the days of pre-ADD diagnoses and ritalin, I was punished severely for my sojourns around the classroom and for my loquaciousness.

One hyperactive, freckled, red-haired boy in a fifth grade class was talking so much that I had to give him a five minute time out. When I talked to him in the hallway about his behavior, he was surprised when I told him that even though his behavior was disruptive, he was a good boy.

He vehemently disagreed telling me that it's not true; that he's a really bad person. He informed me that he's always been getting into trouble ever since first grade. I continued to praise

Mother hugging one of her little children

him, differentiating between his behavior and who he was as a human being. I looked him in the eye and repeated, "You're good. You're really good. You're such a good person."

Suddenly I noticed tears streaming down his cheeks as he cried, "No one has ever told me that I'm good."

He looked up hopefully and asked, "Am I really good?"

I nodded as I smiled down at the little boy. I felt God's grace flowing through me, touching the heart of the unappreciated child.

MOTHER'S LESSON ABOUT THE PROPER USE OF MANTRAS

Although I received a mantra from Mother in 1991 I have had a difficult time trying to remember to repeat it. I even bought a *japa* ring (a ring which helps one remember to repeat a mantra). However, the ring usually circumambulates my finger to the repetition of such inane thoughts as: "Will there be cauliflower for dinner again tonight?; How much will a new radiator cost for my car?; Is it worth it to pay more money for a faster internet connection?"

I have remembered to repeat my mantra occasionally; like the time that the big back hoe I was driving started to tip over as I was backing down a hill or when I had go to the oral surgeon to have a tooth pulled.

When Big Swamiji stayed at the M.A. Center in the Spring of 2000, the residents began regularly repeating the *mahamritajaya* mantra which is a very inspiring Sanskrit mantra. The words mean:

> *"We offer our worship to the fragrant three-eyed Lord Shiva who confers ever increasing prosperity. Please liberate us from the hands of death as effortlessly as a cucumber is separated from the vine. Kindly do not turn us away from liberation."*

I was actually able to sit for long periods of time, in spite of my hyperactive mind, repeating the mesmerizing words. I even found myself repeating the mantra frequently throughout the day.

The following summer I enthusiastically asked Amma for her blessings that I would be able to keep repeating the mahamritajaya mantra. I thought that she would be happy that her mantra-impaired son was finally repeating a Sanskrit mantra.

However, I was quite surprised by Amma's response, "Stick with the mantra that Mother gave you. It's the nature of the mind to always seek new things. The mind is like a bird on a ship. It will fly North, South, East and West; but in the end it will end up at the same place on the sail of the ship. Eventually the mind will become bored and concentration will lesson even with the mahamritajaya mantra. Do the mantra that the guru initiated you in. After receiving a mantra from the queen bee why try other mantras? However, you can do the mahamritajaya mantra for five minutes a day if you want."

Mother teaches the devotees about statue worship

Chittaranjan and Priya, devotees of Amma, bought a large, magnificent, life-like statue of Laxshmi when they were in India, which Mother agreed to bless in San Ramon. Several devotees excitedly waited at Mother's house after a morning program in June 2001 in anticipation of Amma performing a puja (ceremony) for the statue. Priya was holding a lovely silver tray with a candle, flower petals and water for Mother to bless the majestic statue.

When Mother entered the foyer she had a pensive look on her face when she was asked to bless the statue. She suddenly exclaimed, "No formal worship, no formal worship. Do not do the 108 names to the statue. This is an idol. If you worship this statue you would awaken the life force within it. If you failed to continuously perform daily worship, you would anger the life force within the statue and it would lash out at you, like a baby who doesn't get fed daily. It could hurt you as well as future generations."

Similarly Mother once told the residents several years ago that there are subtle beings who are very eager to listen to bhajans. She mentioned that if the ashram residents stop singing to God, it would also create some negative reactions.

Mother, being one with the divine, chose to do a puja. She lit the candles on the decorative tray and performed a beautiful ceremony. She put the rose petals delicately and carefully on the Laxshmi statue after which she held the hands of the statue most lovingly. Finally, Mother put a garland on the statue's neck as she smiled deeply at Laxshmi. She instructed the owners to treat the idol as a work of art, but that it was o.k. to kiss the statue's feet thinking of Amma. According to Swamini Krishnamrita, Mother's puja took away any negative vibrations that the owners unknowingly may have created by having worshipped the statue. Amma is very particular that pujas must be done every day at the Brahmasthanam temples she's inaugurated in India.

Mother discusses how to deal with the ego

During a satsang the ashram residents participated in with Amma in the summer of 2000, I asked Mother, "Can I ask a question about the ego?"

Mother then started laughing as she responded, "This battle of the ego began a long time ago. Even at the times of the Bhagavad Gita (an ancient scripture of India) it was there. Nobody is able to get rid of the ego."

I replied, "I have the feeling I've been battling with the ego for a half century."

"You are old?" Mother inquired.

I answered, "It sure feels old. Mother frequently states that people suffer because they did not get enough love and attention when they were children. I am trying to get attention now that I did not receive as a child to make myself feel better, and this attention unfortunately seems to feed my ego. However, on a spiritual path I'm supposed to be humble, believing that I'm nothing; that everything comes from God. How do I resolve this conflict and release the ego?"

Mother replied, "Do not look at the situation in this way. When there is no awareness there is no knowledge. Till the awareness comes we need love. But this will happen slowly, like salt melting in the seawater. Then this negative feeling will disappear. There was a guru who was teaching his disciples about *maya* (illusion); that everything is maya. At that moment a mad elephant started coming towards them. Everybody including the guru started to run. Later the disciples asked the guru why he was running. He answered that the elephant coming and guru running is also maya. In fact the guru running was the greatest maya of all. So rather than holding onto the past we should look for practical solutions and move forward."

Become a zero and you're a hero

One day when I was doing my lap seva position (helping people going up for a hug from Amma), I felt everything was going smoothly and was quite proud of myself that there had been no major difficulties. However, after about an hour, a man came up to me and whispered in my ear that I needed to pull my pants up because when I would get up my shirt didn't reach down over my loose fitting pants. The other devotees sitting around Amma unfortunately noticed this faux pas, and as I tried to tighten my belt everyone started laughing. Mother noticed everyone giggling and joined in with the hilarity when she saw me struggling, frantically trying to raise my pants. Instead of gazing at Mother's enchanting, divine form, the devotees had a lovely view of part of my naked posterior. Ah, another opportunity to learn humility.

Sometimes performing the lap seva duties is absolutely overwhelming. One morning when I was attempting to do my job correctly, the crowds were extremely large due to the fact that Mother had been on the news the previous night. A bus of handicapped people had just arrived, so I had to help fifteen disabled people who were either on crutches or in wheelchairs to approach Amma.

At one point, an elderly woman suddenly appeared at the front of the line needing help and looking very unstable on her feet. I got up abruptly, tripping over the couple that was receiving darshan and falling flat on my back with my arms and legs straight up in the air. Fortuitously, I didn't land on anyone during my sudden descent. Mother raised her hands in the air to indicate: "What in the world is going on?" She then began laughing hysterically at my pathetic body that was sprawled out in the middle of the darshan line like a dog on its back. As I struggled to crawl back to my lap position with my bruised elbow and ego, I noticed that the elderly lady was returning to her seat easily without anyone's assistance. It seems that Mother will never miss a chance to work on my ego.

Many years ago when I first began doing lap seva, Amma would frequently scold me for doing a poor job. While it's emotionally challenging to be scolded, I considered it a great blessing to have a great mahatma like Amma molding me like a baker kneading dough. I remember one time many years ago watching Amma, the blacksmith, hammering away at the piece of iron named Swami Dayamrita. She kept telling all the devotees how incompetent he was as she made him continue translating for her while he was lying on the ground. He has told me that this training by Amma has really helped him to grow spiritually and emotionally. She was preparing him for a very challenging future job, the general manager of the M.A. Center and Mother's swami for the United States.

On another occasion, Amma told me that she wanted to stagger the devotees coming up for darshan with ten people entering from the front line and five people coming up from both side rows. I rigorously enforced this rule, asking other devotees to help me with the count to double check that I was doing the job correctly. Suddenly Mother got upset with me telling me that too many people were coming up from the center line. At that point I totally lost it and forgot that I was talking to the Divine Mother of the Universe, a Satguru whose consciousness is one with God. I exasperatedly shouted, "Now just wait one minute. You said ten from the center and five from the side rows and that's exactly what I've been doing. Isn't that what you want?"

Amma coyly shrugged her shoulders and responded with a little, mischievous smile, "I don't know." So much for trying to win an argument with God.

During another particularly exasperating lap seva shift on a very hot summer day, I got to the point that I actually couldn't wait to leave. I couldn't tolerate the intensity, scolding and chaos any longer! I decided that I never wanted to do the lap position again. Finally, Bipin, a very calm and compassionate Malayalam-speaking man, *pranamed* (bowed) to Amma and sat next to me. I thought to myself, "Thank God, Bipin's here to replace me. I'm out of here."

I then quickly got up in my perspiration-soaked Indian shirt as I wiped sweat from my brow with my wet handkerchief. I virtually sprinted toward the door in anticipation of buying a refreshing Hansen's soda and a large chocolate-chip cookie in the snack shop. As I hurried toward the door, I visualized myself lying on the grass in the cool shade enjoying my snacks. All of the sudden, I heard my name being called and turned around and noticed Bipin, Swamiji and Mother all waving me back. "Oh no, what the heck is going on?" I thought to myself.

When I reluctantly returned, Bipin told me that Mother requested that he sit next to me so that he could translate for Amma when I made mistakes.

During yet another momentous occasion doing lap seva, when I noticed an old friend, Geoff, in the darshan line a thought popped into my head, "Wow, this will really impress Geoff when he comes up to receive darshan and sees me serving my guru in such a coveted position. I sure hope Amma doesn't embarrass me in front of him." I felt that I was doing a good job that morning so I really had nothing to worry about. However, as soon as my friend sat down next to Mother and myself, Amma told me to make sure that the line moves quickly. Since I had already been requesting the devotees in line to move forward rapidly, I responded, "I know."

She then sarcastically repeated what I mentioned gazing toward my friend, "I know, I know, I know. I know it all." Mother telling Geoff what a know-it-all I am must have really impressed him.

Mother frequently changes the rules of the game to help us learn detachment and to understand that God, not our small egos, is really in charge. For many tours, one devotee supervised all the lap seva positions and would meet with each person prior to their shift. The manager would have little cards to represent devotees receiving darshan and the sevites would practice with each other how to direct people to Amma.

Finally, it felt like the important seva jobs of helping the darshan line run smoothly were finally well organized. Each person who had one of the ten jobs on the men's and women's side had to be at the meeting on time, thirty minutes before their shift began or they would not be allowed to perform their special assignment.

Suddenly, during the November 2000 tour in the Bay Area, Mother exclaimed, "We don't need so many line seva jobs." She dismissed everyone except the lap and exit person, yet the darshan line continued in an efficient fashion.

Breaking down the writer's ego

It can be very dangerous for the ego of a spiritual aspirant to write a book, since maya can delude the author into thinking, "What a great and spiritually uplifitng book 'I' wrote." When my first book about Amma was published in November 1997, many devotees including some of the swamis asked me a multitude of questions about the book. I was finally getting the attention and recognition that I always craved as a child, as well as receiving positive feedback from many people about my accomplishment.

However, the only person whom I was really interested in getting praise from for doing a good job was the Divine Mother. As I slowly approached Amma in the question line with a copy of my book, I decided to ask her to bless the manuscript so that the stories might help inspire many devotees on their spiritual path. I became quite excited wondering how Amma would respond to my new book, remembering how she enthusiastically shouted, "Yes, yes, yes" when I asked for permission to write the book.

Finally, I eagerly approached Amma and handed her the book requesting that she bless it. She unexpectedly responded sternly, demanding, "Did you get approval from the board before you wrote this book?"

"Well, Swami Paramatmananda read it," I meekly replied.

"What about the other board members?" she tersely inquired.

"They were aware that I was writing the book," I desperately answered.

After a few moments she emphatically stated, "Mother will bless the book, but you should have gotten permission from the board of directors first."

Realizing the danger of increasing my ego that would further stunt my spiritual growth, Mother in her compassion, didn't praise my effort. I remember hearing once how Mother was going to praise one of her close disciples, but then chose not to give her accolades, as she mentioned that she wanted that daughter to merge with God.

After one evening program during Amma's November 2000 visit, one devotee came up to me with tears in her eyes exclaiming, "Dayalu, I just read your book and it was so inspiring. I had been a devotee of both Yogananda and Amma and after reading your book, I now understand my relationship with both saints. Thank you so much."

I then started feeling pretty darn good about myself. "Boy, I've sure helped a lot of people," I thought to myself. Less than a minute after the person who complimented me walked away, another devotee strolled up to me and enthusiastically stated, "I really enjoyed the satsang that you gave tonight. I found what you had to say about marriage very helpful and inspiring. Thank you so much."

Startled by the unearned compliments, I responded, "Thanks, but it wasn't me. It was Bernie who gave the talk tonight and we look a little bit alike evidently." Ah, Amma never misses an opportunity to deflate the devotee's ego.

HAPPY BIRTHDAY TO YOU, HAPPY BIRTHDAY TO YOU, HAPPY BIRTHDAY DEAR EGO

Although I experienced quite a challenging childhood, my birthdays were always extremely enjoyable. My mother used to treat me with special love and attention and I could do no wrong that day. As an adult I have always tried to recapture the joy and the feeling of being special on my birthday.

However, many people who live in an ashram feel that celebrating one's birthday only serves to bolster the ego. "Everyone look at me; I'm special. Everybody acknowledge me and sing to me. Today's 'my day.'"

Part of me feels that there's nothing wrong in receiving special love and attention on one's birthday. Perhaps the key is to spiritualize that special day by creating a special *satsang* (spiritual gathering) with soul-stirring bhajans and prayers which can create divine blessings, rather than just indulging the ego with a candle-laden cake, saturated fatty ice-cream and a banal birthday song.

I don't particularly like cakes but I really have a craving for pies, so on my birthday a few years ago I requested someone in the ashram to make a fruit pie. However, when I returned to the ashram twenty minutes late after dinner, I was dismayed to find everyone finishing off my birthday cherry pie which definitely did not make me cheery.

During another birthday in the ashram, it was so obvious that a few people were preparing a party that I needed to hide out in the hallway so a few residents could complete the usual preparations. When I was asked to enter the kitchen, I needed to utilize all my acting ability to appear surprised as the lights dimmed and the flaming candles on the cake were carried into the kitchen.

I remember many years ago that one resident asked Swami Paramatmananda if she should celebrate her birthday. She was so upset about not knowing what to do. He responded, "Since just thinking about it is creating so much frustration and mental disharmony for you, perhaps it's best not to celebrate your birthday."

A new ashram resident, Avinash, was born the day before me so some devotees had secretly planned a double birthday celebration for both of us. This secret plan was truly an ingenious surprise party since I was instructed to come to Avinash's birthday party the night before my birthday. Unfortunately, I had other plans that night and when I returned to my room rather late that evening, I found it strange that there were five messages on my answering machine pleading with me to come to Avinash's birthday party.

The next morning I discovered that many people attended the double birthday party for Avinash and myself and that both our cakes had been eaten. However, when I came up to the main house for lunch the following day, I still secretly hoped that I would be acknowledged with a little celebration just for me. After waiting around for over an hour until everyone finished eating lunch, I decided to return to my room. Just as I was walking out the door, a few people came into the kitchen singing happy birthday with a lone candle squashed into a remaining scrap of day-old cake that one thoughtful resident was able to salvage from the previous night.

Unfortunately, when other residents asked for their cake, someone yelled out that all the deserts had been scarfed down the day before. I then sat down by myself on the cold, linoleum floor as the other hungry, disgruntled residents left the kitchen. As I sat by myself holding a Mickey Mouse balloon, I read greetings on my special birthday card such as, "Dear Avinash, I'm so glad you moved into the ashram last year," or "Dear Avinash, Happy 32nd year." (I should be so lucky). Occasionally I found a message addressed to Dayalu.

Through these birthday lessons, Mother has helped me to realize that since the soul is ageless, I shouldn't focus on receiving tributes from other people as the years of this incarnation quickly evaporate like the morning dew. Even if I were given a grand birthday celebration, the temporary love and attention would fade by the next day. I'd rather celebrate the soul's ability to merge with God instead of fleeting recognition and sugary praise for the impermanent body that will be reduced to a box of ashes in a few years.

Mother shows her ego

During one tour I decided to explain to Amma why I never have come to Amritapuri. I revealed to her that the reason I don't visit India is due to the fact that I have a neurological disability that makes it really arduous for me to be in a noisy place.

I was stunned when Mother furiously began shaking her finger at me and forcefully demanded, "What about all the noise in your head? Once you master that, you can go anywhere in the world. Now, your mind is like a giant monkey jumping from branch to branch."

Suddenly, Mother bit her finger as she was pointing at me, but then softly added, "Even Amma showed ego when she was pointing her finger at you. That is why she bit her finger."

I responded, "If that's the case, I should probably bite both my fingers."

She laughingly replied, "You need to bite all of your fingers and toes."

I then awkwardly tried to shove my hands and feet into my mouth to the laughter of Amma, Big Swamiji and the devotees in the darshan hall.

Of course, Mother, whose consciousness is one with God, has no ego. However, just to teach me a lesson, she pretended that she had an ego. She bit her finger to show me how egotistical I behave whenever I point an accusatory finger at someone else. After all, when I'm pointing one finger at another person, three other fingers are pointing back at me.

CHAPTER III

More lessons on tour with Amma

"A true Master will never use his power for any destructive purpose. He always uses it for the good of the world and for the upliftment of society. But remember that he can also use it to teach the entire human race a lesson. A Self-Realized Master is one with the Cosmic Energy, and that energy is infinite. He can release it or hold it or do whatever he wishes with it. He can choose to release either positive or negative energy. But even if he should release it in a seemingly negative way, it is only for the good of the world; it is done only for the sake of teaching someone a lesson."

ASKING MOTHER A QUESTION ON TOUR

Many people ask Amma a question, secretly hoping that she will respond in a way that will satisfy their ego. Unfortunately, when Mother doesn't give the devotee an answer that they want to hear, they often rationalize that either Mother doesn't really understand the question or else they simply ignore her advice altogether. It is very important not to ask Amma a question unless you're ready to follow her advice implicitly.

The ego has a way of twisting Mother's words and actions to fit its own desires. I'm astounded how many people have become such proficient interpreters of Amma. I've been told:

"Mother told me that I should be a renunciate as reverse psychology because she really wants me to live a more spiritual life with my girlfriend."

"I'm not going to take the job Amma told me to take because I know that she just said that because she really wants me to make my own vocational decisions. Therefore, I'll stick with my current job."

"I know the reason Amma looked at me with a smile when I was sitting in the back of the crowded hall was just to give me a special sign to let me know that it is alright to sell my possessions and move to India."

"Mother didn't answer my question about my marital problem when I asked her during darshan, to let me know that I was intuitively right in wanting to divorce my husband."

"Mother pretended not to notice me as she was getting into her car which really meant that it was o.k. for me to meet with her after darshan."

"Amma came to me in a dream and told me it was o.k. for me to sleep in the temple since I don't have money for a motel."

In one tragic incident, a devotee asked Mother what to do about a catastrophic disease that she was suddenly diagnosed with. Mother gave her specific advice regarding the type of treatment she should follow. Unfortunately, the devotee chose to pursue a different healing modality. When her condition severely worsened, she asked Mother again what she should do. Mother simply told her that she couldn't recommend anything at that point since she didn't follow Mother's instructions initially.

Frequently, the more specific a disciple's question, the clearer the advice is. Sometimes it's important for the devotee to clarify what Mother means if her response seems too general. Several years ago I asked Amma if I should move out of the ashram. She responded "Do as you wish."

At that point I responded, "No Mother, Dayalu's will is your will. I will only do as you wish."

She then added, "If you move out of the ashram you would eventually cease to exist spiritually."

However, another time she told me that it would be o.k. if I moved out of the ashram as long as I lived nearby. The advice that Mother gives is specific for the devotee at that particular time.

In a similar incident many years ago, a friend of mine, Pavitra, asked if she should move into the ashram and Mother responded, "Do whatever you like."

However, my friend persevered with further clarification inquiring, "What is the best course to take for my spiritual growth?"

Amma finally responded, "It would be best if you lived in the ashram for your spiritual growth."

Flying with Amma

Every year since 1993 I've been blessed to share several airplane flights with Amma. All the devotees hope to get a seat near Mother, and consequently, a few years ago I arrived early at the Seattle airport gate where a seat would be assigned to me. Unfortunately, I arrived at the gate too early and was told to come back later to obtain my seat assignment. I went to the ticket counter several more times, but was still not able to reserve my seat. I became worried that since the flight was very crowded all the seats may have already been assigned. My goal at that point was just to obtain any seat on the plane.

When Amma arrived at the gate, I became mesmerized standing in Amma's presence. I forgot to return to the ticket counter to ask for my seat assignment again. Suddenly, I realized that it was getting close to departure time, so I extracted myself from Mother's holy presence and ran to the ticket agent. As I feared, the airline representative told me that all the seats had been assigned. I became frightened that I would not be on the flight with Amma and I began worrying how I would get to the San Ramon ashram from the airport on a later flight. As the devotees began boarding the plane, the agent called me to the counter and informed me that there was room for me in first class and within minutes I fortuitously found myself sitting a few rows in front of Amma.

I didn't want to bother Mother, but I really wanted to ask her to pray for my dad who had just sustained a debilitating stroke and was confined to a nursing home. I asked Swamiji if I could ask Mother this question. Amma's non-verbal response was simply to give me a very long, compassionate look. Standing in the aisle with the Holy Mother's tender gaze enveloping me for a few moments, I felt like my body was melting into the floor.

Out of the blue, she unexpectedly asked me, "How is your headache?"

I answered, "I don't have a headache and I rarely get headaches."

She then inquired, "Isn't there some problem with your head?"

I mentioned that she is always putting sandalwood paste on my forehead when I receive darshan because of too much heat in my head. After a few moments she gave me a long, loving hug.

I blissfully returned to my row and as I maneuvered into my seat, all of the sudden, smash, bang, pow! I smacked my head on the overhead luggage rack. Swamiji smiled as I painfully responded rubbing the side of my head, "Now, I've got the headache."

Who knows what karma Mother speeded up, released or modified through this incident? Even with a slight bump on my head, I joyfully gazed at the snow-covered peak of Mt. Shasta and the magnificent green forests below. As my eyes focused on the shimmering pinnacle of the mountain, all I could see was Mother's compassionate gaze enveloping me.

A trip to the airport with Amma

The morning Amma was leaving San Rafael, California after the November 2000 tour, I happened to be at the house where Mother was staying since I needed to talk to one of the swamis. A woman stopped by in a van and said she was going to lead the way for Mother to go to Judith Cornell's house for a home visit. (Judith Cornell had just written the new biography of Amma). Since the devotee with a truck never showed up to get Mother's and the swamis' luggage, a few of us began loading the baggage into the van.

Mother unexpectedly came out of her room and proceeded to get into Ron's car an hour before her scheduled departure. As Mother's car backed down the driveway, I bowed and waved goodbye to Amma since it would be my last view of her during this visit. Out of the corner of my eye, I saw Ramakrishna Swami and Kamal (an Indian man who travels with Mother) running down the steep driveway yelling "Dayalu, where's your car? Quick we have to follow Ron. We're supposed to go on the house visit with Mother."

Just then Amritatmananda Swami yelled from the porch, "Dayalu, wait, we need to put luggage in your car since the truck didn't come."

Not knowing which swami's direction to follow, I suddenly came down with a bad case of "swami-stressitis." Since Ramakrishna Swami was standing right next to me and I figured that I could call someone to pick up the luggage on my cell phone, I would drive Ramakrishna Swami to Mother's house visit. Ramakrishna Swami and Kamal immediately jumped into my car, landing on the pre-teen toys strewn all over my car seats. As my esteemed passengers were removing plastic battleships, dice and 'go directly to jail' cards from their dhotis, Ramakrishna Swami yelled, "Hurry, hurry, follow Ron's car."

I looked up helplessly at Amritatmananda Swami who was standing on the deck looking bewildered as to where I was going, as I hit the gas pedal. I sped down the suburban streets as fast as I could trying to catch up to Mother's car, repeating my mantra and praying that I wouldn't get into an accident or receive a 'go directly to jail' card myself. As I ascended the ramp to the freeway, Ramakrishna Swami asked, "Can't you get the car to go faster?"

I told him that my old Toyota just didn't go as fast as Ron's new car. However, on a downhill section of the freeway, I was able to catch up to the elusive gold Lexus. "Wow," I thought, as I arrived at Judith's house, "I get to go on a home visit with Amma."

Unfortunately, I spent most of the time on the phone trying to arrange for someone to pick up the luggage. However, at one point I entered the living room where Amma had already served the devotees prasad. I noticed there was some apple pie, my favorite desert, and hoped I could discretely grab a piece before I left for the airport. Unexpectedly, Amma looked at me, cut a piece of pie and handed it to me. "How sweet," I thought, as I put the scrumptious morsels in my mouth that had just been handed to me by the Divine Mother.

I was informed that Mother's flight was scheduled to depart at 2:45 P.M. from San Francisco airport and I noticed that it was already 1:45. I told Ron and Big Swamiji that Mother should leave immediately since it can take forty-five minutes to get to the airport. Ron told me that he wasn't sure how to get to the airport from San Rafael and that he would follow me. I thought that this would really be fun "leading" the Divine Mother to the airport. I became thrilled with my new important position. However, on the way I suddenly became nervous and frightened as I tried to remember the shortest route to the airport.

I looked into my rear view mirror as I turned right a few blocks from Judith's house. To my horror, Ron who was several cars behind me must not have seen me and turned left. I thought, "Oh no! There's no freeway entrance in the direction that he's driving. I should have pulled over and let the other cars behind me pass so he would have seen my car more clearly. He'll never make it to the airport on time and Amma will miss her plane. It will be all my fault when Amma doesn't show up in Michigan with hundreds of devotees waiting for her."

I became panic-stricken not knowing how to remedy this horrendous situation that I created. I kept obsessing on the bad karma that I had just accrued by losing Amma's car. I was replaying in my mind how I should have told Ron the directions before we left.

About thirty minutes later, while stopped at a traffic light in San Francisco, I noticed a gold Lexus to my right and joyfully beheld Mother chatting with Big Swamiji. I then calmly led Ron to the airport. Upon arriving at the terminal, I was surprised that there was no one in front of the terminal to greet Amma since it was now only twenty minutes before Amma's flight was scheduled to leave. After we quickly let Mother and the swamis out of our cars, Ron asked me if we should park the cars to see Amma off at the gate. I told him that the flight was leaving soon so we wouldn't make it to the gate in time.

I drove off feeling satisfied that I didn't bungle Mother's ride to the airport and that I was able to spend a few minutes with her during the intimate house visit. However, much to my chagrin, I later found out that Mother's flight was really scheduled for an hour later and even that flight was cancelled, so Amma gave satsang for the lucky devotees in the airport for over an hour.

Overcoming challenges on tour in San Ramon

Many years ago I wrote my doctoral dissertation on the psychological and physiological effects of meditation and the physical isolation tank on Type A behavior (characterized by always rushing, competitiveness, multi-tasking and hostility). I've heard it frequently repeated that you teach what you need to learn, and so in writing my dissertation, I was really searching for new ways that I could modify my hyperactive Type A personality.

During the tours in San Ramon, my fifty-five square foot office/bedroom needs to be vacated, since my room is used for childcare. During the 1999 tour, I was able to jam my little desk, file cabinet and phone into an overcrowded, stifling-hot, windowless yurt (a tent-like structure). I shared the dilapidated, leaky tent/office with several devotees. The yurt was located in my backyard, which is used as the children's playground during tour. Anyone who has seen Amma in San Ramon is aware that the M.A. Center is not exactly a bastion of peace and tranquillity with thousands of people roaming around the property in a carnival-like atmosphere.

Since 1996 I've been teaching classes on stress reduction and a local newspaper reporter had contacted me requesting an interview about reducing stress. Although I tried to decline giving the interview during tour, the reporter was persistent so I finally relented, agreeing to a phone interview.

Although the reporter was under the impression that she was interviewing me at Dr. Zeff's plush office in San Ramon, little did she realize that the interview was actually taking place from a Hindu ashram in a smelly, disheveled tent that was situated in the middle of a children's playground with hundreds of people walking by.

When the reporter questioned me regarding what techniques I personally used to stay calm, I began a long soliloquy on the importance of meditation. In a very calm and peaceful voice, I discussed the importance of watching the thoughts rather than over-reacting to external stimuli.

As I continued my rather pompous speech on the importance of staying centered, suddenly, several children began screaming a few feet from the yurt as a group of teenagers sitting in a nearby car started blasting rap music. I very politely and calmly asked the reporter to please hold on for a minute as I sprinted outside and told the children to go play somewhere else informing them emphatically, "I'm trying to conduct an important interview."

I then ran over to the car filled with the teens and shouted at them to turn the music off. I then screamed with my face turning red, "This is an ashram, not a rap concert hall. I'm trying to give an interview on how to stay calm."

I scurried back to the phone, breathing heavily and wiping my brow with my sweat-soaked Amma T-shirt. I continued disseminating professional advice to the reporter about the importance of staying centered in a phony, tranquil voice. I completed the interview with one hand over my ear and sweat profusely pouring down my face. At the end of the stressful conversation, I was grateful that at least the interview wasn't completed in person as I pondered how Mother invariably sets up situations to help me look at my hypocritical behavior.

During Mother's visit to San Ramon in November 2001, I stored all of my valuable possessions in a small, locked room in the tin barn. One of the biggest challenges for me during tour is that I have to move all of my possessions out of my room twice a year. One drizzly night I returned to the locked room in the barn to return some equipment that I used for the childcare program. To my horror, I found my computer, printer, and the manuscript of this book, as well as all of my valuable possessions lying heaped in a pile outside of the room.

My office is located near the Temple

Through a series of miscommunications, someone accidentally threw my valuables outside. In my usual calm and centered manner, I totally freaked out, ranting and raving as I was forced to move my precious possessions to another room at midnight in the rain. At that point, I felt it wasn't worth it to continue living in the ashram. I'm simply too attached to my "things" and too hypersensitive to continue living in such a chaotic situation.

The following day when I went up for darshan during Devi Bhava I felt so dejected that I felt I had lost faith in Mother. However, during the darshan, Amma seemed to pour her divine love into every pour of my body and filled me with effulgent bliss. It was perhaps the most blissful darshan I had ever experienced from Amma in thirteen years. When I sat down to meditate, my only thought was "living in the ashram was worth every bit of frustration I experienced." In retrospect, through Mother's grace, I have become less attached to my material possessions. The worldly desires pale in comparison to the depth of divine bliss that Mother showers upon the devotee.

Most devotees have no problem falling asleep on a floor crammed into a small room with ten other people. However, I tend to wake up with every little noise that I hear and then have a lot of trouble falling back asleep. I tried sleeping under crowded conditions at a few retreats, but found that I didn't get any sleep and couldn't function well the following day. Consequently, several years ago I slept in a tent during one San Ramon tour. While it was uncomfortable sleeping amongst ticks, spiders and mosquitoes on the hard ground, at least it was fairly quiet. A week earlier I had also slept in a tent in a campground at the retreat in Fort Flagler near Seattle. Unfortunately, I awoke on the first morning of that retreat in a pool of freezing water with a soaked sleeping bag. But at least it was quiet.

In the afternoons in San Ramon when I wanted to take a nap, the tent would become overheated in the direct sun light during the day, but at night it would become quite cold. Perhaps due to my bone-chilling experience at Fort Flagler, I came down with a flu a few days after the San Ramon program began. That night I tried to fall asleep on the cold, hard ground but found myself unable to breathe whenever I lay down. As the night progressed, I developed chills and a fever. By the following morning I discovered that my temperature had risen to 104 degrees and my entire body was aching. Although I was shaking from the chills, I was simultaneously perspiring and my clothes were soaked.

Since I had to give up my room during the tour, I kept most of my possessions in my car. I couldn't rest in the overheated, sundrenched tent during the following day, so I deliriously packed my few remaining possessions in my car and drove to a nearby shopping center in San Ramon. I curled up in the back seat of my overheated car and rolled down the windows to try to catch a breeze that would hopefully lower my temperature. All of my crumpled clothes and self-improvement books were carelessly stacked to the roof in my old, dust-covered Toyota. I noticed some of the nouveau riche, matronly shoppers who were adorned in gold jewelry and wearing five-inch high heels staring at me in disgust as they entered Neiman-Marcus. I thought to myself, "This is as bad as it could get. I was broke, homeless and now living out of my car, suffering with a very high fever."

With sweat and tears flowing down my face, I cried out to Amma to help me. Suddenly, I thought of calling some friends, Scott and Meridian, who lived in Berkeley. They kindly allowed me to sleep on their living room floor. As I slowly trudged up the stairs to their apartment carrying my few possessions, I realized how grateful I felt for being able to have some floor space in a living room. I reminisced that a few years ago when I was earning a good income, I could have stayed at a nice hotel if I were sick. Today's wealthy man can easily become tomorrow's pauper. The ebb and flow of the waves of prosperity and poverty in this short life can change in a moment like the wind in a storm.

The following week when I felt well enough to attend the programs, Amma, noticing me sitting in the temple, compassionately asked me if I was feeling better. I was so touched by her kindness that tears welled up in my eyes as I gazed into Amma's translucent, sparkling, brown eyes that morning. My soul yearned to merge into Mother's eternal light and love. Who else is there for me but you, Amma, my refuge and protector?

Kali's sword

On the first morning of the Chicago program, July 4th 2001, it seemed as if every Indian family who lived in the Chicago metropolitan area showed up for a blessing. By 10 A.M. over 1000 darshan tokens had been distributed and the morning program didn't end until close to 5 P.M.

I wanted my niece, Rebecca, to receive a special blessing from Amma that morning, but due to the huge crowds and innumerable amount of families, her blessing was very short. As soon as she and her friend were blessed, they left the hall and decided not to return for the evening program.

About an hour later I noticed that Mother seemed to be experiencing pain and had asked for some experienced people to help out with the darshan line. One devotee came up to me and said, "Dayalu, you've done lap seva a lot. You should go up there to help out." Noticing that Amma seemed to be in a *Kali bhava* (the mood of the fierce goddess of destruction and transformation), I was reticent to help out with the line. However, the person in charge of the lap seva told me that I should supervise the devotees doing the lap seva on the men's side. I noticed that the sevites who were helping the devotees exit after receiving darshan were inexperienced and a few times they were pulling devotees away, while Amma was simultaneously pulling them up for darshan.

Reluctantly, I began helping with the lap seva. It wasn't long before Amma reached down to bring someone up from the men's side for darshan and there was no one there so Amma fiercely shouted at me, "Move back!"

Shaking with fear, I quickly retreated and made sure that there would always be someone waiting to get blessed on the men's side when Mother reached down for a devotee. A teenage boy came up for darshan with his dad. After the boy received darshan, I quickly moved him behind his dad so that the two of them could be blessed together and to make room for the next devotee on deck. However, after Amma blessed the dad she pulled the boy back for a second blessing and was upset that he was far away from her. She then screamed at me in Malayalam with the full wrath of Kali. As I trembled with fear and dread, the translator shouted at me, "Mother says for you to go sit on the side." I was fired by the Divine Mother.

While I was initially devastated over what happened, I later realized what a blessing it was to have so much fierce energy from God directed toward my soul. I pondered, "This is actually quite an incredible opportunity to realize how insignificant I really am. I had the audacity to believe that I was really important supervising the line, which resulted in a wake up call by Amma."

Even though I realized what a spiritual boon it was to have experienced Kali's wrath, I began feeling that I was really incompetent and worthless and berated myself for causing Mother so much inconvenience. A few hours later I remembered that I had to discuss some ashram business with Dayamrita Swami, so I waited for him in the swami's suite in the hotel. Suddenly I heard a booming, deep voice shout, "Dayalu, Dayalu." I looked in the various rooms until I found Big Swamiji sitting in front of a lap top computer. He had just written an essay about *Guru Poornima* (an auspicious annual holiday honoring the guru during the full moon) that would be listed on the Ammachi web site and asked me to edit the story.

Who me? Dayalu, the nincompoop who Mother just kicked off the stage for messing up the darshan line? However, I felt honored as I acquiesced to Swamiji's request. I nervously reviewed the text and made some editing suggestions trying to be most careful not to make another blunder that day. Swamiji humbly thanked me for my help and I slowly began to feel that I may not be totally worthless after all. My emotions around Amma tend to resemble a roller coaster; perhaps Amma should have named me Dayayoyo.

During the evening bhajans my soul's yearning for God wouldn't allow the earlier traumatic experience to dilute my love for the Holy Mother. Singing with my full heart yearning for God, I realized that regardless whether Mother appears as Kali cutting my ego with her sword or as Devi wiping away my tears with her compassion, I always want to keep sipping her *amrita* (divine nectar) from the straw that can bring my soul eternal Bliss.

The following night during Devi Bhava, I became quite tired around two in the morning and decided not to stay till the end of the program, so I drove an hour to my niece's house in downtown Chicago. I was a little disappointed that my niece, Rebecca, didn't attend the evening program the previous night, but decided not to push her to see Amma again. Rebecca had told me that recently she was working on the 10th step in her twelve-step program, which focused on how to experience God in your daily life.

When I returned to Rebecca's house at 3 A.M., my niece was still awake and suddenly asked me if she could get a mantra during Devi Bhava. I told her that if she wanted to go to Devi Bhava she would still have time to get a mantra from Amma. To my surprise, she immediately drove to the program, arriving in time to receive a final blessing from Amma.

While she was getting blessed, she asked Amma for a mantra. However, Amma was busy talking to someone else and didn't respond. She then decided to go right home, but as she was leaving the stage several people came running up to her saying that Amma wanted Rebecca to sit next to her. When Rebecca returned home the next morning carrying many bhajan tapes and Amma books, she was saturated with Amma's love, excitedly informing me, "Uncle Dayalu, I want to go to India. I want to know what all the words mean in the tapes I just bought. How can I get a copy of the 108 names of Amma?" Thank you Kali for letting my niece experience your bliss.

Chapter IV

The Bliss of God and Amma

"Each one runs after his own happiness. God is of the nature of bliss and we can only live happily if we live in God. Therefore, if we merge in the Supreme Truth, we can always experience bliss. Even if all the people in the world were to love us, even then, we would not get an infinitesimal amount of the bliss that we get from God's Love. Try for that Eternal bliss in the time that is remaining. A Satguru is the very source of eternal bliss and happiness."

Mother is with you when you sing bhajans with your heart

I've experienced that Amma has come to me when I have sung bhajans with devotion and concentration. When Big Swamiji came to stay in San Ramon for a few months in the winter and Spring of 2000, he gave many spiritually enlightening classes. For example, he informed the devotees that the word aum is actually three syllables: a, u, m, which represents Brahma, Vishnu, and Shiva; the creator, sustainer and destroyer. He also mentioned that Amma told him that the spiritual path is not really a movement forward. We are actually going backwards toward the source and in that process we have to experience the emotions from many births. However, Amma is always present, guiding and protecting the devotees when we are experiencing the vasanas. Therefore, we will always get through any difficult situation just like the sun that sets every night.

Each evening Swamiji would sing awe-inspiring bhajans. One of my favorite songs is "Kamesha Vamakshi Kamade," which I hadn't heard for a long time. Some of the words to this

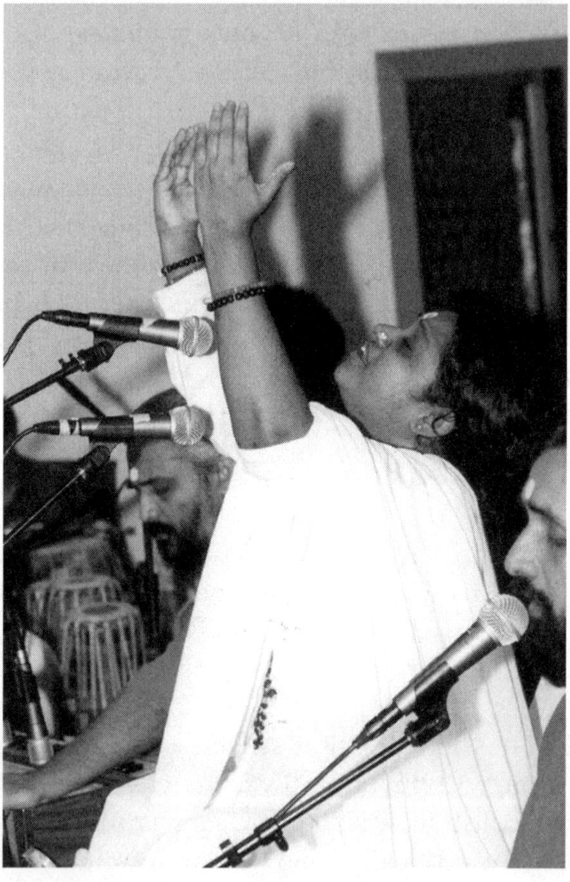

Amma ecstatically singing to God during bhajans

rousing song are "Salutations to Shakti, the great Goddess who is accessible through devotion, salutations to the one Seed, the one Truth, the infinite perfect Awareness. Thou art the Veda, the Absolute, living beings and salvation too."

The intense rhythm and melody of this song can reach a feverish pitch that has uplifted me to an ecstatic state. I had asked Swamiji if he could play the song one evening. That night when he played this devotional song, I felt my body and mind become enraptured in divine bliss. As I sang while meditating on Amma's beatific form, I suddenly started smelling the scent of roses that Amma emanates. As the divine aroma became more intense, I felt Mother's presence sitting along side me in the ashram puja room and realized that Mother is always with me when I call out to her with an open heart.

A BLISSFUL EXPERIENCE

During the November 2000 tour I was reflecting that it had been many years since my last transcendent, blissful experience in Amma's presence. My two highest and most enlightening experiences had occurred during Devi Bhava years ago. That year during Devi Bhava in San Rafael, I was asked to do prasad seva handing Mother flower petals and chocolate. However, there were many people waiting to give prasad and I really wanted to eat dinner before I did my lap shift seva, which was scheduled an hour later. I asked a person in line if I could go in front of her. This request created quite a disturbance and when it was finally my turn to get near Amma to give prasad, I became confused. I mistakenly gave Mother chocolate instead of flower petals. I realized my mistake as the candy bounced back off my head and someone else handed her flower petals. I felt disgusted with myself and felt that I didn't deserve to do lap or prasad seva. I became very scared that Mother would berate me during my lap shift for my egotistical behavior of trying to push my way to the front of the prasad line.

However, perhaps since I approached Amma with humility, the lap shift went smoothly. After being so close to the Goddess Devi for quite a while, I felt the divine energy saturating every cell of my body. I sat down to meditate and spontaneously went into a blissful state: a feeling of such divine joy surging through me… I can hear sounds and chatter in the background, but for once it does not affect me… like noise from some far off place that has nothing to do with me… this state is so different from the Earth plane… like being in heaven…Mother-Father-God emanating pure unconditional love rises up within me and embraces me... I float outside and marvel at the stars, the sky, the perfection of the Universe that I long to merge back into…my body dissolves and I'm free again in Thy Light...total peace and serenity…peace and

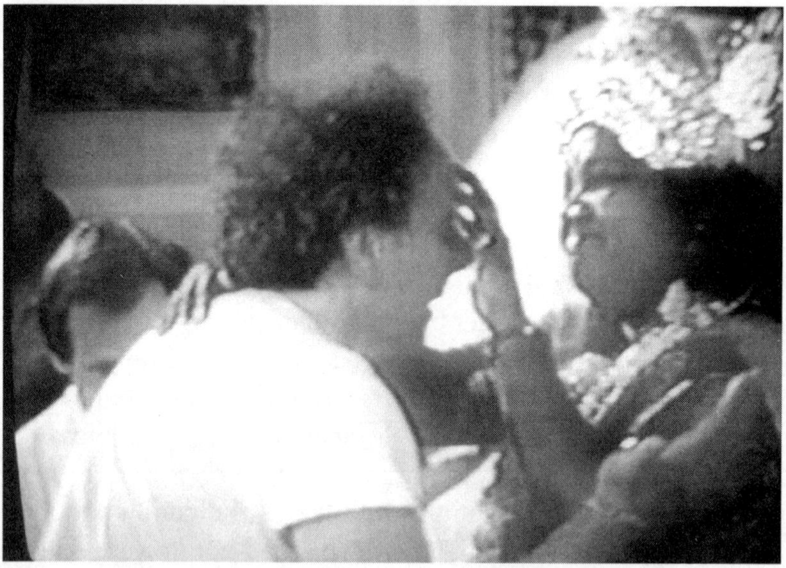

Dayalu receiving a blessing from Amma during Devi Bhava

serenity…stillness…aliveness…I smell the sweet aromatic scent of thousands of roses surrounding me…. Oh Beloved Amma, bring me home to the other shore of existence…save me from the grip of maya…"

The blissful state lasted for over an hour. When I returned home that night, full of joy I wrote: "It's difficult for me to light a match in the windy rainstorm of life. Amma, please light my divine spark. Only your flame from God can relieve my sorrows and stop my unfocused mind from wandering aimlessly in the never-ending cycle of birth and death. Please let your divine light ever glow within me. Let the glimpse of divine bliss that you have graciously bestowed upon me tonight motivate me to use all of my strength and will-power to merge into thy divine love forever and ever."

Mother's internal blessing can be more powerful than her external touch

Since I have trouble functioning with little sleep, I finally found a way to attend the spiritually dramatic conclusion of Devi Bhava, which usually takes place between 5 and 7 A.M. I now take a very long nap from 1:00 A.M. till 4 or 5 A.M. Unfortunately, during the first Devi Bhava in San Ramon during the 2000 tour, I thought the program would end later than it did. I hadn't yet received a darshan from Amma in San Ramon and really wanted a hug. As I rushed into the hall at 5 A.M., I was surprised to see that Mother was giving her last darshan to a man in a wheel chair and that a couple was standing on stage waiting for Mother to marry them. I went up on the stage hoping that there may be other devotees whom Mother hadn't yet blessed, but unfortunately the man in the wheelchair was the last person in line. I told one of Amma's assistants that I didn't get darshan and she asked me to move in front. However, I didn't feel comfortable receiving darshan in front of everyone as Mother was getting ready to perform a marriage so I decided not to receive a blessing. Besides, I thought to myself, "Hadn't I received enough Devi Bhava darshans over the last thirteen years?"

At the conclusion of Devi Bhava, after Amma showered the devotees with flower petals, I was able to sit in front of the Divine Mother in all her glory. She was dressed in a sparkling yellow sari, wearing a pure white garland around her lovely neck as she showered a rainbow of flower petals on the devotees. When the curtains closed and the final prayers ended, virtually everyone in the hall began talking and mingling, as they waited in eager anticipation of seeing Amma leave the hall.

Amma in deep meditation

However, I was transfixed in a deep meditation, as I felt waves of bliss flowing up and down my spine. I thought, "Maybe this is what Mother means when she says I'm always with you." Although I was aware of hundreds of people pushing toward the back of the hall to get one more glimpse of Amma as she exited the temple, I returned to my meditation, feeling content that I was truly visualizing the eternal Divine Mother. That spiritual joy was much deeper and more profound than any outward, blissful experience I have ever had gazing at Mother's physical presence.

As I slowly arose an hour later from my bliss-filled meditation, I thought of Amma's New Year's message for the millennium: "We can never expect that anything will change externally. The real change has to come from within us. The stench of the negativity is within us. Our ego, jealousy, greed, anger and selfishness have to go. We have to fill our hearts with the fragrance of love, compassion and patience. Let us step into the new millennium with this goal in mind."

God in Nature

When I teach classes on stress reduction, I emphasize how important it is for people to spend time in nature to awaken our natural *sattvic* (harmonious) qualities. Prior to living in the M.A. Center in the Bay Area, I resided for eleven years in the Sierra Mountains in Northern California. For my first thirty-seven years I had always lived in urban environments, so when I moved to very rural Nevada County, it was quite an initial adjustment. However, my body, mind and soul soon relaxed in the peace of God's natural environment. When I have lived in a city, I become deluded believing that it's natural to sit in traffic jams on freeways, inhale toxic pollution and listen to cars honking. However, when I spend time in a bucolic, pastoral environment, I feel my connection to the Divine Mother more deeply. Every year I try to spend a few weeks in the mountains which helps me to connect with my true nature.

On one recent trip to the Sierra Mountains, I sat down in a half-lotus posture to meditate on top of a lookout tower with a 360 degree view. I gazed at the bright snow-peaked mountains; the lush, velvet, green valleys; the strong, giant pine trees; the majestic azure sky above and the powder-white cloud formations. I beheld the absolute perfection of the Universe all around me. As I slowly breathed this effulgent scene into every cell of my body, I felt myself merging into the divine creation. I felt as if I were just a little bubble that wanted to return to my eternal home.

The following day I journeyed to the river where I observed a cornucopia of multi-colored flowers covering the hillside above the foamy, cascading water. I witnessed yellows, reds, oranges and purples all bursting forth from the Creator. The aqua-blue river below me was rushing over giant, gray boulders, which reminded me of the soul flowing toward the source.

I approached the river and lay down on the soft, white sand. I noticed a yellow butterfly, its wings displaying an intricate design of black dots, delicately land a few inches from my head. I marveled at the perfection surrounding me. As I stood under a powerfully flowing waterfall, I prayed, "Amma, cleanse my mind of impurity and negativity. Let your divine power purify my body, mind and soul."

Suddenly, everywhere I looked I saw God. The Divine Mother was everywhere: in the flowing waterfall; the colossal rocks; the dazzling, white sand; the towering, green trees; the warm, soft sun on my back; the crystal-clear, eternal blue sky. I spontaneously began shouting, "God, God, God," as I waded into the river, and floated on my back on the gentle currents that were meandering through the canyon.

I sang out with joy, "God, you are my father, mother, friend and creator. You reside everywhere." Since both my parents have now passed away, I then thought of the words of a song that the Indian saint, Parmahansa Yogananda, had frequently sung,"'Father, Mother have I none. I am He, I am He, blessed spirit I am He.' Other than you, beloved God, who is there to look after me? You are my source, my rock and my redeemer."

From Dreaming to Waking: Synchronicity in the Divine Search

When I lived in San Francisco in the 1970's, I once visited a house that was for sale. I always wanted to own my own home, which I had believed would give me a feeling of security. However, even home owners are really renters in this transitory world of maya. When it is our time to leave the body, we have to give up the deed to our earthly home, as well as all of our impermanent possessions.

Twenty-five years ago when the real estate agent showed me through the vintage San Francisco home, I remembered suddenly being consumed by an eerie sense of déjà vu. The hillside residence was a quaint, blue and white Victorian home that was built before the turn of the century and had survived the 1906 earthquake. I was fascinated by the fact that though the house looked like a small, two-story abode, there were many stairways that descended deeper and deeper toward three levels located beneath the ground floor.

For the last twenty-five years I would periodically have dreams that I was living in that house. The dreams may have represented delving deeper into the subconscious from a Jungian perspective, or perhaps I had actually lived in that house in a past life. I'm not sure why I kept having the recurring dreams, but I do remember some inexplicable feeling of safety and inner-peace during my nocturnal sojourns, as I descended deeper toward the bottom layers of the house.

One night several years ago, I had another very realistic dream of living in that same Victorian house. When I awoke that morning, I felt disoriented. Was I in a room in the ashram or in my multi-level hillside home? Later that day, I found myself with an extra hour to spend in San Francisco before I had to pick up some ashram residents at the San Francisco airport. I inexplicably found myself driving toward the house of my dreams. I luckily found a parking space on the hilly street and walked toward the brightly-colored house with the cupola and bay windows. As I approached the home, a friendly lady in her mid-50's, dressed in a tweed business suit, suddenly came walking up to me from the porch of "my" house and enthusiastically exclaimed, "I've been expecting you. Won't you come in?"

I was rather shocked by the invitation and didn't know if I was in a repeat of the television show the "Twilight Zone," or just dreaming. When the smiling woman saw my bewilderment and hesitation, she asked, "Aren't you the man who called the real estate office who is interested in viewing the house for sale?"

Evidently another man was supposed to have shown up at the exact time to see the hillside house which had just been put on the real estate market for the first time in twenty-five years. As I walked through the house, the real estate agent was surprised when I described the rooms in detail before we entered each one. However, after I viewed the entire house, it felt like some vasana had been removed since I never had another dream about the house after that visit. It felt like Amma had taken away the attachment to the nineteenth century home to help me live more in the present.

Last year I had read two books that dealt with guardian angels and subsequently began having several dreams where I felt some undefined, mysterious, angelic energy enter my consciousness. While the ultimate guardian angel is my beloved Amma, I understand that there may be angels from the other side who are also here to protect me and help me grow spiritually. I began having a strong desire to contact my personal guardian angel in meditation, but I knew that it would be a most arduous task given my hyperactive mind. While I have meditated daily for almost twenty years, most of my meditations seem as shallow as a dried-up creek bed.

My pathetic morning *sadhana* (spiritual practice) consists of mentally repeating my mantra, perhaps twice if I'm lucky, before I focus on really important spiritual matters such as pondering the great truths of life, like, "Is it better for me to eat hot cereal or eggs for breakfast? If I have the eggs, I'll be getting more protein, but eggs have cholesterol… but then it will take longer to clean the pan and since I'm sharing my house with so many people the bathroom may not be available later… Oh, I should have gotten gas at the cheaper station yesterday and saved four cents a gallon, times ten gallons would be forty cents I would have saved…I need to remind myself to ask Avinash to help me repair my computer…I don't know why the screen keeps freezing. Maybe I shouldn't have sold my old Mac...If I make $200 a week substitute teaching, that should pay for room and board but then I'll need at least two astrology readings a week to earn enough each month… I should do more seva or people will think I'm a slacker… but I do more seva than some of the residents and I try to go to the evening programs which looks good… wow, thirty minutes are up already… oh yeah, oṃ shanti shanti shanti."

In order to have my mind focus on something spiritual during meditation for a change that day, I decided to pray to God to reveal my guardian angel. Even with my short-term spiritual memory loss during meditation, I somehow forced myself to continuously ask Amma and God to reveal my guardian angel. After some thirty minutes of almost incessant praying, I felt a bright light penetrating my spiritual eye. I slowly opened my eyes and beheld a luminescent light shining from the top of my large crystal located in front of a large picture of Mother in Devi Bhava. Even if I couldn't contact a specific angel, in my heart I felt that I was always protected by Mother's angelic energy. Later that afternoon I went to see a touching movie entitled "Pay it Forward," which, unbeknownst to me, turned out to be about angels. At the end of the movie a song began playing in the background entitled, "Calling all Angels." With Amma's grace, when I disciplined myself to concentrate during meditation that day, I received angelic energy.

Mother frequently tells the devotees that it is important to use self-discipline when you meditate. She told the ashram residents during a satsang several years ago, "When you meditate with concentration on the guru, who is one with the universal mind, the energy will come back to you as grace. It is just like the heart pumping blood throughout the body. The impure blood returns to the heart where it will be purified."

I have often had experiences of feeling connected with Mother through dreams. After Mother left the United States in November 2000, she visited Kuwait for the first time. On November 29th I had a dream that the sound system wasn't working when Amma was singing bhajans during a program in the Arab country. The devotees were desperately trying to fix the equipment so that the thousands of people could hear Mother's sweet voice. Since the dream was particularly vivid, I jotted down my night's reverie in my journal the following morning.

Swamiji later told me that on the same night that I had my dream, the devotees were worried because the Kuwaiti police had confiscated the sound system of another group that rented the same hall a week earlier. He also informed me that some devotees were trying to repair the sound system, which was malfunctioning and Swamiji was concerned that there might not be any bhajans. However, when the police came to the hall that night and heard Amma singing to God in her melodious voice, they left the hall without interfering with the repaired sound system. Since the disciple's soul is deeply connected to Amma, at times we may be able to subtly tune into her energy wherever Mother is staying on the Earth plane.

Amma singing bhajans

In December of 2000, Amma came to me in a dream and told me that beginning February 11, 2002 there could be a significant change in my life. Later when I looked at my astrology chart, I realized that would be the exact day that I would finish an inauspicious Ketu lunar node period and begin an auspicious Venus planetary cycle. Interestingly, two months after the dream on February 11th, 2001 would be the day of my dad's funeral. Perhaps Amma was also preparing me on a subtle level for my father's passing.

One of my seva duties in the ashram has been performing tractor work, which I really enjoy but can be dangerous. The tractor driver needs to be alert at all times, which is a good opportunity to practice shraddha. My growing up in a Jewish suburb and attending graduate school in psychology wasn't exactly the best training for a future heavy equipment operator in a Hindu ashram. While attending Hebrew school, the urban adolescents didn't have to move horse manure with the front loader like some boys who were raised on a farm in the Midwest. Jewish young men are instructed from an early age to use their mind to study, not their hands to grease the bolts on a back hoe.

Devotees using the tractor to complete a Saturday seva project

There isn't a strong propensity for most Jewish psychologists to spend their weekends filling a dump truck with horse poop. Consequently, I can understand why my dad wasn't so impressed with my newly acquired skill, when I told him years ago of how I spent my avocational time. He preferred to tell his friends about his son the Ph.D. psychologist, so I could understand when he replied with some disdain, "Oy veh, my son the tractor driver."

In spite of my lack of training and innate non-mechanical ability as a heavy equipment operator, I have persevered in performing this seva. One night during the winter of 2001, I had a dream that I was driving a tractor that was running out of control down a steep hill. Every attempt that I frantically made to try to stop the tractor was fruitless, and ultimately the tractor crashed into a huge, white wall. I woke up abruptly, sweating profusely and with my heart racing. The dream was very realistic and upon awaking, I remembered that in a few hours I was scheduled to grade the muddy road leading into the ashram. I tried to calm myself down by thinking that it was only a dream and that I was safe since I was only going to be working on a flat surface.

The next morning as I turned on the tractor and began doing my seva, I totally forgot about the dream. I saw a friend walking by whom I needed to speak to, so I quickly jumped off the tractor to catch up with him. After a few moments I intuitively turned around, and to my horror, I saw the tractor rolling toward the white barn. Instinctively, I sprinted toward the heavy machinery, quickly mounting it and slamming on the brakes. The tractor jerked to a stop only a foot before it would have smashed into the white wall. As I breathed a sigh of relief, I suddenly remembered the dream. I felt that Amma's grace prevented a major accident by my having gone through the accident in the dream.

CHAPTER V

There is no Death

"This is only a rented body. At some point, we will be asked to leave it. Then we must go out. Before we leave, that which is eternal should be gained while residing in this body. If we have a house of our own, we can happily move out when we are asked to vacate this rented one. Then we can live in the eternal house of God.

The pain of death is caused by the thought that death is going to destroy everything that you have-all that you are attached to and all that you cling to. That clinging causes the pain. If only you can let go of all your attachments, then the pain of death will turn into an experience of bliss.

Death is not complete annihilation. It is a pause. It is like pressing the pause button on a tape recorder in the middle of a song. Sooner or later, when pressed again, the pause button is released and the song continues. Death is only a period of preparation before the start of another life. You unpack your content only to re-pack it in a fresh new package, in which the ingredients will be the same."

Why Amma rarely intervenes in our karma

I used to think that Amma would intervene in a person's karma and always heal the devotees who are very sick. However, in order for the devotees to make spiritual progress, sometimes Mother heals people, yet other times for the devotees to grow spiritually, she chooses not to heal them. When we get a body, it's inevitable that we get a problem. No body, no problem.

When my dad had a stroke in April, 2000, I told Amma that I felt so sad seeing him lying helpless in a nursing home. Amma responded, "Mother can't interfere with your dad's poor physical condition. He needs to burn off his karma. If Amma intervened, it would upset the laws of nature. However, you can pray and Amma will also pray for your dad."

Furthermore, Amma rarely intervenes with a devotee's emotional karma. I've had a challenge during this incarnation with my hypersensitivity to noise. A few years ago a friend of mine told me about a new machine that could change my brain waves, eliminating my noise sensitivity. Even though the high tech treatment was expensive, I was desperate. I asked Amma if I should try the new technique before I spent thousands of dollars and a great deal of time trying to change my "karma." Her response was not very enthusiastic. Her omniscient reply was, "These things usually don't work." Amma was subtly informing me that it was best for my spiritual growth to accept my hypersensitivity to noise.

I actually wasn't surprised by Amma's response, since, as an astrologer, I understand that the auspicious and inauspicious planetary alignment in each person's chart is based on the karma from previous incarnations. I've never seen a malefic planet disappear from a birth chart, which would eliminate a specific karma. Mother's grace can help a devotee cope with inauspicious events that arise in a person's life. Also, performing *puja* (ritual worship), prayer and mantra definitely helps lessen any malefic planetary alignment.

My chart is extremely inauspicious for having a long-term, successful marriage. In our society virtually everyone is conditioned to believe that they will only be content if they live happily ever after with their soul mate. In spite of the fact that many marriages end in divorce or are frequently unhappy, most people still feel that their happiness is dependent on having a loving, intimate relationship with another person.

One of the most important benefits that I've received from living in Amma's ashram over the last six years is letting go of the need to have an external relationship to feel peaceful. I've noticed that the more that I surrender to my fate during this brief incarnation, rather than fighting the effects of my astrological chart, the happier I become.

When I recently entered a Ketu astrological period that has brought some physical challenges, I simply acknowledged, "Here comes Ketu again."

I realized that for a limited time period, I was supposed to have physical problems. I can just imagine the karma I've created through my deeds and actions in this short life, let alone in hundreds of previous births. This information helps me understand why there is so much emotional and physical suffering.

The direct guidance of a Satguru will guide us through challenging astrological time periods. A few years ago I was experiencing some physical challenges during a Saturn period and I asked Amma specifically how I could cope with my health problems. She compassionately gave me the following specific advice, "Stick to a regular routine, eat less fatty foods and oil, eat a lot of vegetables and fiber, exercise regularly, receive gentle massage and meditate daily. You don't have anything serious and Mother will help with your physical condition. Repeating affirmations will also help, such as 'I am full of energy.' You can also take ayurvedic herbs."

When I accept the planetary alignment for this incarnation, I also don't have to become so egotistically attached to my few abilities. For example, if someone compliments me on my writing, I know that it's just the placement of my Mercury and Sun that created this aptitude and that has nothing to do with "me." Recently, when someone mentioned that it must feel good to be wanted when I was asked to lead the ashram meetings, I responded it's not "me" that they want, it's just my Sun in the second house that is sought after.

The Transition of Amma's Close Disciples

The first close Western devotee of Amma to pass away was Bramacharini Nirmalamrita in 1999. She was a *bramacharini* (renunciate) who had worn yellow, which signifies the step prior to becoming a swami or swamini. This very kind, tall, dark-haired woman always had a supportive word and smile for everyone. She had returned to the M.A. Center from Amritapuri in March to help prepare for the retreats during the summer tour.

The ashram residents were deeply concerned when one night Nirmalamrita was rushed to the hospital. She had had cancer many years ago, but was healthy since she met Amma twelve years earlier. Unfortunately, the dormant cancer had reappeared and spread to different parts of her body. The ashramites performed continuous archana and prayed for her deeply. As she lay dying in a hospital in Oakland a few weeks later, Mother consoled her by calling from India and gently saying, "Darling daughter, take my hand and I will lead you into the garden."

At the time, I was initially very saddened and surprised that Mother didn't intervene to save her life. After Bramacharini Nirmalamrita passed away, Amma once mentioned that she could feel her presence stronger than when she was in the body. It was evidently the time for Nirmalamrita to grow closer spiritually to Amma in the subtle plane.

Bramacharini Nirmalamrita with Amma

A friend of mine had a dream about Nirmalamrita a few weeks after she left her body. In the dream Nirmalamrita's soul related that she was in a place that was like Mother's etheric ashram. Nirmalamrita described to my friend, "The only difference between the two of us is that you can visit both worlds but I can no longer be in a physical form."

My friend suddenly woke up and excitedly wrote down the information that Nirmalamrita's soul conveyed to her. When she went back to sleep, Nirmalamrita reappeared and continued, "As

I was saying before you woke up," and then proceeded to share with my friend her experiences in Mother's astral ashram.

When Amma was in Japan at the beginning of the 2001 tour, she received sad news that Amit, one of the most beloved brahmacharis in Amritapuri, was suddenly killed in a car crash. Amma, as the Mother of Compassion, wept for her son, who just left his body crying out, "Why did you leave Mother?"

However, a few days later when she arrived in Seattle, Mother said she beheld Amit's smiling face and felt closer to him now than when he was in the body. She also asked some of the swamis, "How long could I keep saving him?"- implying that she had already intervened in postponing his destiny. She had told Amit not to drive a car before she left India but the karma was so strong that when a devotee in Amritapuri refused to give him a car, he secured another vehicle for his trip to the Aims Hospital in Cochin.

When Amma returned to India, she said that many people had been jealous of Amit but that he did not have a mean bone in his body. She planted a sapling tree in the ground with his ashes. Mother further suggested that she hoped that the people who were jealous of him would sit under the tree and benefit from the vibration of the purity of the tree.

One close devotee of Amma's was brought to her in a wheel chair during darshan November of 1999. Elizabeth was near death as the cancer she had been battling for years finally had begun spreading throughout her body. As she told Amma about her severe pain and deep fears, Elizabeth began crying uncontrollably. Mother wiped away the dying woman's teardrops with her sari as Amma's eyes welled up with tears of compassion. As both devotee and guru held each other, intertwined in a stream of tears, it seemed as if the fragile devotee's soul was merging in a river of salt water toward God. When Elizabeth passed away a few weeks later, I remembered the poignant scene in the temple and was sure that Mother was taking good care of her daughter in the etheric plane.

I'm beginning to understand that it's not as important how long my friends, loved ones or myself continue living in the body, as much as that we are all growing spiritually. As I learn to accept my karma, I realize that the real help Amma is giving me isn't necessarily a long, healthy life, but helping my soul evolve spiritually. I once told Mother that I hoped that the astral plane wouldn't be as difficult as the suffering I've experienced on the Earth plane. She responded, "As long as you hold on to Mother's feet, you will have nothing to worry about in the astral plane." Guru charanam Satguru charanam, Amritanandamayi charanam...The guru's feet will give us refuge.

THE COMPLETION OF MY DOG KARMA

Of the many stories that I shared in my last book, one that people seemed to be very touched by dealt with my dog, Shalom. Thirty years ago I acquired a little black mutt with brown spots and floppy ears who was to eventually become a source of unconditional love for me for sixteen years. In 1992 I asked Amma, "Would you pray for my dog who left her body six years ago?" I had hoped that Mother would simply respond that she would pray for the dog's soul in the etheric plane.

However, her answer really surprised me. Ammachi replied, "She is now a girl almost five years old who will become a devotee; a strong believer in God in her life!"

Mother wouldn't say where this little girl was living. How incredible that my puppy dog that I'd been mourning for had been transformed into a five year old girl. If my dog was reincarnated as a five year old child, there truly is no death! What a great example of maya! For years I was melancholy about missing Shalom, when in reality she was a little girl, possibly even residing in my neighborhood! It was good that I didn't find out where she was currently living because I'm sure the parents would have been horrified if I showed them pictures of what their cute little girl looked like a few years earlier or worse yet, if they had earlier seen me walking their "daughter" on a leash in the neighborhood!

Amma rarely tells devotees what happened to the soul of their relatives, let alone pets that have passed away. Many people have come up to me over the last few years, teary-eyed, to discuss the fate of their deceased pet who had given them unconditional love. One lady even asked me if I thought her beloved pet hamster would become a human.

Even though I had to find a new home for my second dog, a big, friendly, black hound named Karma, when I moved into the ashram in February of 1996, I was able to visit him on a regular basis since he lived nearby. A spiritual teacher had predicted that three months after my dog Shalom died, another dog would be waiting for me on my doorstep. Sure enough a few months after my first dog died, I moved into a new house in 1987 where my "Karma" was waiting for me.

Dayalu feeding his new friends, the swans at the M.A. *Center. What will these birds become in their next incarnation?*

Karma used to like to imitate both my good and bad habits. I was often surprised to find Karma sitting with his eyes gazing at my pictures of Amma in a dog pose-*asana* (hatha yoga posture) in front of my altar when I entered my little puja room. On one occasion my dog Karma had the good karma of receiving prasad from Amma.

One yoga posture I excelled in at home was the couch-potato pose. I would lay on my back in a mutated form of *sarvasana* (posture lying relaxed on one's back) in the living room, reading or watching television while continuously eating which created great flexibility in my right arm. I used to be surprised to find Karma also lying on his back on my living room couch munching my junk food that he had grabbed off the top shelves of my pantry. He could have at least gobbled the delicacies quickly in the kitchen like most dogs, instead of imitating my indolent asanas.

I have practiced vedic astrology for years, but am continually astounded at how accurate this science is in predicting both auspicious and inauspicious time periods. I noticed that on September 14th 2000 I was going to begin an emotionally difficult time period related to loss. I got a call that day that my dog fell down and couldn't get up. However, Karma's caretaker said that she couldn't get an appointment with the vet until the following morning. I told the caretaker that I would meet her at the vet's office the next day.

I felt that it was my fifteen year old dog's time to leave his body. He had been getting weaker for the last several months. I didn't sleep well that night feeling that Karma would probably have to be put to sleep the next morning. I brought some food, flower petals and sacred ash to give to my loving companion. When I arrived at the parking lot of the vet's office, the poor dog was in such a critical condition lying in the back of the caretaker's camper that he couldn't move. His eyes were rolled back and his mouth was closed tightly so that he couldn't eat the food I brought him. All I could do for my loyal companion at that point was rub sacred ash over his body, sprinkle rose petals from Amma on his head, and repeat holy mantras in his ear as I stroked his virtually lifeless body.

By the time that we carried my seventy- pound dog into the vet's office on a stretcher, his soul felt like it was virtually out of his body since he hadn't really eaten or drunk anything in more than a day. When I laid his dying body on the examining table, I looked deeply into his eyes for the last time. I stroked him gently and told him that I loved him and that Amma loves him. I quickly returned to my car and began sobbing deeply, thinking of how he lay suffering in the back of the camper for a day in an utterly helpless and painful condition. I was surprised how emotionally upset I became since he really didn't live with me full-time for several years. However, the loss of unconditional love and separation from a dear friend is never easy.

When I returned home I meditated on my dog and felt Karma's soul come to me. I encouraged him to go to Amma and into the light as I stroked his etheric body. However, he seemed to just want to be in my presence an hour after he left his body. Five hours later I meditated again and felt his black, fury essence on the left side of my lap, but this time it felt like I was holding a shell. His soul felt very far away. I then remembered that during my last meditation, I encouraged him to go into Amma's divine light. I then began pondering where his soul went. As soon as that thought popped into my head, I felt a flash of light appear on my eyelids. A burst of sun light streamed into my room covering my face. I called out to the sunbeam, "I love you Karma, go with love. I send you all my blessings."

When I meditated the next morning, I suddenly felt Karma talking to me as if he were a human being. He conveyed to me that he was free now and told me not to worry; to be happy. Abruptly, his energy field became so weak that there was no more contact. Leaving the body may be the ultimate form of jet lag. I reminisced how my other dog emerged like a butterfly from an astral cocoon into a little girl. Forms are continuously being created and dissolving in the world of maya.

A few months after Karma left his body I brought his ashes to the country home where I used to live. My former neighbors Chittaranjan and Priya strolled with me up the hilly property filled with beautiful green pine and majestic, ancient oak trees; the land where Karma used to run like the wind as he joyfully raced through the mountainous forest terrain. As we scattered the dog's ashes over the tall, straw-colored grass singing "Om Namah Shivayah," I realized that in a very short time, someone will be spreading my ashes.

As I meditated a few minutes later, I thought of how most people spend so much time and money trying to look attractive so others will admire their body. They try a multitude of diets, buy stylish clothes, pay beauticians to dye their hair and join pricey health clubs to lift heavy iron objects. I began laughing at the absurdity of how we try to increase our ego by beautifying the body, which is ultimately just a pile of ash.

Upon further contemplation on death, I thought of how we sacrifice our life in order to earn money, status and fame. That morning I had seen a bumper sticker that stated, "the person with the most toys at the end wins." However, the person with the most toys at the end is still dead. There's a beautiful line in a song by the Persian poet Rumi that exemplifies the transitory nature of the body: "You're in your body like a plant that is solid in the ground."

Amma has said, "We should be like a bird perched on a dry twig. While it sits on the twig, it may peck at fruit in the tree, but at the same time it will always be alert and ready to take flight. It knows that any moment the dry twig could snap. The world and its objects are like a dry twig inasmuch as they offer us no lasting support. We must be alert and detached like the bird even while we are in the world. Then we can soar up to the heights of spiritual bliss. We can leave our bodies at any moment and should always be aware of our true nature."

I asked Mother a few months after Karma left his body where the soul of my dog had gone. Perhaps since I was attached to a response like the one she gave me concerning my other dog, Shalom, Mother simply responded, "Amma is not yet aware of where the dog is."

Amma blesses my dad's transition

Many years ago I coerced my dad to receive a blessing from Amma even though he had adamantly resisted going up for darshan.

In retrospect, I've learned that I don't need to drag all of my friends and relatives screaming and kicking to the lotus feet of the Divine Mother. I've come to understand that my acquaintances and family will receive God's blessings through me. It's quite egotistical to think that everyone should see "my" spiritual teacher because she's the highest guru on the Earth. If someone had tried to pressure me to see Amma when I was in my college fraternity when my focus was on drinking beer and partying, I would have told them to get lost since I was definitely not ready for a spiritual experience.

In the last few years I had grown very close to my dad—a short, heavy-set widower who always had a friendly word on his lips for everyone. He was perhaps one of the kindest people I have ever met, the epitome of a gentleman. Although he worked as a social worker for non-profit, Jewish community agencies, he cared about the well-being of everyone and felt that all of humanity was his family. His favorite charity was

Amnesty International which helps victims of torture in countries throughout the world. An intellectual who was devoted to his religion, Judaism, he nonetheless considered himself an agnostic. However, he did acknowledge there was a mystery to life which he couldn't understand and received deep, spiritual inspiration through his enjoyment of classical music, Mozart being among his favorite composers.

My dad's 90th birthday party
(top row left to right) my nephew, Jason; Dayalu; my son, David (bottom row) family friend, Kathy; my sister, Judy; my niece, Rebecca. My dad is seated.

My dad had a stroke a few months after we celebrated his 90th birthday and in the last few months of his life he was frequently rushed to the hospital from his nursing home. Whenever I visited him in these institutions, invariably the staff would tell me how much they loved my dad. While other patients would frequently complain or scream at the nurses, my dad would apologize to them for making such a mess and thank them enthusiastically for all their help.

I flew to New Jersey at the end of January when my dad's doctor informed me that my father only had at most a few more weeks to live. When I arrived at the hospital, I was an emotional basket case. I beheld my once vibrant, healthy and vivacious father lying semi-conscious with oxygen tubes in his nose and IV's hooked up to his arms. His legs had developed a condition similar to gangrene from painful sores due to diabetes, and he just suffered his second congestive heart failure in less than two weeks.

It seemed as if all my spiritual principles that I had been practicing for years were thrown out the window. The Hindu teachings state that it's important to be detached. However, if I am a compassionate human, I will instinctively feel pain and sorrow at the death of a loved one. I don't feel that repressing sadness and keeping a stiff upper-lip helps my healing process. Yet, when I have obsessed on grief for a long period of time, I become depressed. I have found that letting the feelings out is necessary to be able to fully heal and regain spiritual equilibrium.

I was able to send a message to Amma prior to flying to New Jersey asking her to pray for my dad's soul and to give me the strength to deal with his passing. She had responded that her prayers were certainly with my dad and me. I constantly and intimately felt Mother's grace during the last two weeks of my dad's life.

All I could really do for my dad at the hospital was try to feed him, tell the nurse when he needed more morphine and most importantly tell him how much I loved him. Even in my dad's semiconscious state, he was the loving optimist who was always concerned about others. When my son, Dave, called from Colorado, my dad started asking many questions about his job as if he weren't lying in a hospital dying. When my nephew, Jason, and I woke my dad to tell him we were going out for dinner, he cheerfully smiled and weakly whispered, "Have a wonderful time."

After spending a few days visiting dad in the chaotic, antiseptic and unhealing environment of a hospital, he was transferred back to the nursing home on hospice, which meant that the nursing staff would not resuscitate him during his next medical emergency.

I filled the nursing home room with lovely flowers, played recordings of my dad's favorite classical music concertos and read poems from his beloved books of poetry. I tucked my dad in bed with a lovely purple, blue and magenta afghan my grandmother knitted for her young son almost a century earlier. Even though I was sorrowful, I realized the blessed way my dad was leaving his body. A mahatma had prayed for his soul as he rested in a sunny room filled with bouquets emanating sweet scents while listening to grand sonatas surrounded by friends and family telling him how much they loved him.

The following week my dad's condition remained stable, but he still slept most of the day. Even though he was in a deep sleep, I felt that on a subtle level his soul could still hear the uplifting poetry that he cherished throughout his life. I began reading a poem by Edna St. Vincent Millay entitled, "My Candle Burns At Both Ends."

"My candle burns at both ends, it will not last the night,"...suddenly, I heard my dad's voice weakly whispering the rest of the poem by heart, "it will not last the night, but ah my foes, and oh, my friends, it gives a lovely light." While I contemplated that he may not last the night, during his life he had given off such a lovely light as he prepared to go into the omnipresent light of God.

The little glow of the body may be extinguished, but with Amma's grace I prayed that his soul would merge with the eternal light of God. The following morning I was just finishing a very peaceful meditation, when I noticed that a Jewish star appeared at my third eye. The Jewish star is engraved on tombstones in Jewish cemeteries just as a cross is placed on monuments in Christian graveyards. At that moment, the phone rang and my niece, Rebecca, called to tell me that my dad had another congestive heart failure and was in a coma.

The doctor told me that he would probably leave his body in a few hours so I rushed over to the nursing home. He hadn't had food or water for almost twenty-four hours and since he was on the hospice program, the nursing staff could only give him morphine. I anxiously watched as he struggled for air throughout the day, but he continuously kept fighting for one more breath. My sister, Judy, was flying in from St. Louis that evening, so perhaps he was waiting for her to arrive before he made his final exit from his body.

At one point in the afternoon, a visitor came to see my dad who seemed to have a great deal of difficulty accepting my dad's imminent demise. As family and friends gathered around my dad's deathbed, she began nervously talking loudly about her favorite television shows. In a nervous, high-pitched voice she declared, "Well, I like the 'Survivor' series better than the game shows…and 'Who wants to be a Millionaire' seems so contrived with 'Is that your final answer.' "

I found this surrealistic scene quite disturbing, as many of the visitors began loudly discussing the merits of various television shows in front of my dying father. I was trying to create a sacred environment, but didn't feel it was my place to tell the other guests to change the subject. Therefore, I quietly put on my walkman headphones and felt soothed listening to bhajans from Amma's sweet, divine voice. I started singing "Om Namah Shivayah" softly into my dad's ear as I prayed deeply to Amma to help him in his hour of transition. I then prayed deeply that Mother would transform the energy in the room and create a spiritual environment conducive for my dad's imminent transition.

Unexpectedly, a nurse's aide quickly walked up to my dad. As she leaned over his body with tears streaming down her cheeks, she cried, "David, don't you know that everyone loves you? You can let go now."

She then kissed him on the forehead and began sobbing profusely as she left the room. The energy immediately shifted as everyone in the room became quiet and somber. One of the thousand names of the Divine Mother is the one who gives peace and repose to those afflicted with birth, old age and death. It felt like Amma sent the nurse's aide to give comfort to my dad at his time of death. I felt that his soul left the body at that point and I began weeping deeply.

After my sister arrived that night, I decided to leave the nursing home, remembering that dying patients frequently wait until they are alone to leave the body. However, my niece and nephew decided to stay with dad all night. I sadly whispered my final goodbye to my dad thanking him for being such an inspiring and kind person. I softly repeated some prayers in Hebrew and Sanskrit in his ear, kissed him goodbye as I spontaneously bowed to him on the white, linoleum floor.

When I returned home exhausted, I immediately fell into a deep sleep only to awaken a few hours later with an excruciating pain in my left leg. During the last few weeks of his life, my dad complained of the severe pain that his nearly gangrenous open wounds on his left leg caused him. The sharp pain in my leg was almost unbearable, but it only lasted for about a minute.

As soon as the pain dissipated, I felt myself floating in space being drawn toward a deep, luminescent blue and silver light. It was the most indescribably beautiful vision that I had ever beheld. Simultaneously, a deep feeling of freedom and joy enveloped my entire being. After some time in this blissful state, I realized that my dad must have just left his body. I fell back asleep and my nephew, Jason, called me in the early morning to tell me that my dad passed away at 12:30 A.M. which was the exact time that I experienced my astral journey to that enchanting *loka* (world).

During my morning meditation, I had a vision of my dad's soul deep inside the sparkling blue and silver loka. It appeared as if he were reviewing something. Then I heard his calm, gentle voice declare, "It's the darndest thing, Ted, I'm here but also there at the same time."

I could feel his presence strongly for the next twenty-four hours and the following morning in meditation when I told him that I was going to his funeral, I felt his response in his usual optimistic manner, "Enjoy, enjoy."

The next day my dad's soul seemed very far away as if a veil descended preventing me from contacting him anymore. Even though I wasn't able to be in touch with his soul, an e-mail that I received from Big Swamiji helped me realize that his soul would be in peace through Amma's grace. Swamiji wrote, "May our beloved Amma shower her choicest blessings on your dad's soul and uplift him to the highest level of consciousness where he will abide in the light of Amma's divine love."

A few months later when I saw Amma, she corroborated my experience of observing my dad ascend to a beautiful world. She told me, "Your dad is in a very beautiful world and is very happy there." When I asked her if she could describe what it is like for him in the astral plane, she added, "It's like soap bubbles rising; each bubble is a different beautiful color. Your dad's soul is floating from one world to another."

The night after the funeral when I returned to the ashram I was feeling that I really needed a hug or some direct connection from Amma. I wanted to be held and comforted by the Divine Mother. In a dream that night, Amma came to me. I asked her questions about the nature of death and she proceeded to tell me a story from the Bhagavad Gita which assuaged my fear of death. I remember looking into her luminous eyes and a deep sense of calmness pervaded my soul. I woke up feeling peaceful and content. I now understood that when the disciple calls out to Amma from the depth of his or her heart, the Holy Mother will always comfort the devotee.

Two months after my dad's passing, my sister called and told me that a man contacted her declaring that my dad had pledged $10,000 to a non-profit organization and requested the money. My first reaction was quite negative. Why would someone ask for a large sum of money now that my dad had passed away? Since my dad was very generous, he may have made the pledge, yet I wasn't sure what to do.

That night when I want to sleep my dad appeared in a dream. During this extraordinary dream, he appeared as real as when he was in the body! We looked deeply into each other's eyes for a few minutes as if we were transfixed for a moment in eternity. I then reached out to him to touch his hand. He simply responded, "Look…my leg doesn't hurt anymore. I have no pain."

I was awe-struck by the longing in his eyes. For a few moments it looked as if he were trying to tell me something, but suddenly his image faded. I woke up with my heart racing, realizing that what I just experienced wasn't merely a dream. His soul really came to me and wanted to tell me something; probably about what I should do regarding the financial pledge, but his soul departed before he could tell me what to do.

Although I have a difficult time focusing in meditation, the following morning I deeply called out to Amma in meditation to ask her to reveal answers to some questions I had. Surprisingly, I received a clear message. In response to the question about giving money to the non-profit agency, I felt her response, "If the money is going to a good purpose and your dad's signature is on the pledge, you can give the money."

Amazingly, Amma told me in person two months later virtually the identical answer,"If the pledge was in writing with his signature, you can give the money."

Amma discourages devotees from focusing on the astral plane since she wants people to improve themselves in the here and now. It's very easy to be deluded talking about past lives and trying to contact astral entities. Many years ago I had taken a workshop in channeling and was quite frightened when an entity had taken over my vocal cords and I began speaking in a supercilious British accent. The entity told me that the instrument was afraid, but not to worry since the entity would depart at the end of the session.

Even though Mother told me what to do about the money which the man from the non-profit organization requested, I still had a desire to contact my dad's soul. A friend of mine was learning how to channel souls from the astral plane and I foolishly asked if she could contact my dad as a medium.

As I sat on a comfortable couch with sage burning and a small candle glowing in the center of the room, I was mesmerized by incessant drumming that would call forth the spirit of my dad.

A voice came through the medium's vocal cords that sharply announced that he was my dad. The voice indicated that he never realized how much he loved me and was sad that he never expressed his love to me. I became teary-eyed hoping that the spirit was really my dad talking to me from the astral plane. However, after the entity made some statements that clearly indicated to me that he was an imposter, I told him that I didn't think he was my dad. At that moment, the entity immediately left the room.

The medium was very disturbed that a negative entity had entered the room and the other people at the séance also felt that it wasn't my dad speaking through the medium. Later the medium called back the "imposter" spirit and asked him why he came. The entity indicated that he overheard the conversation before the session and hoped that the medium could help him. The people at the seance sent him healing energy so that he could go into the light rather than being stuck on the Earth plane. This experience convinced me how dangerous it is to dabble in seances and reinforced my belief that I should only either pray to Amma or ask Amma directly any questions I have about departed souls. Only an omniscient Satguru has the ability to help us understand the complexities of issues dealing with departed loved ones.

A RATIONALIST OPENS HIS HEART

When I visited Mother in New York City in July of 2000, I stayed with my former brother-in-law, Stan, in his small Manhattan apartment. He would normally never have considered seeing a Hindu guru since he had been an agnostic and rationalist throughout his fifty-seven years. However, he was suffering with colon cancer, which had been spreading throughout his body, even after many treatments of chemotherapy. As Stan dealt with his catastrophic illness, I noticed that he had become more open-minded. In the classes that I have taught on stress reduction, I tell my students that usually the only people who are open to modifying their Type A behavior are post-coronary heart patients.

Even though my scientific and skeptical former brother-in-law agreed to receive darshan, he was reticent to enter the special needs line although he was in a weakened condition. When he received his blessing, Prem, the medical doctor who administers the AIMS hospital in India, was translating for Amma. When I told Prem about Stan's current medical condition, Mother looked horrified and asked many questions about the disease. She gave him a very special, long hug and when he returned to his seat, he was beaming and grinning from ear to ear. He kept repeating that she had held him so tightly. On a subtle level, it appeared that she had really touched his soul, regardless of the effect it would have on his medical condition.

Exactly one month after my dad passed away, Stan died after his two year struggle with cancer. On the morning that Stan left his body, I meditated and prayed for his soul. However, when I tuned into his energy, I felt that he was initially in a very confused and fearful state surrounded by dark energy. I urged him to go into the light; go to Amma, the lady who hugged you so tightly.

After I finished my meditation, I was able to get a message to Amma to ask her to pray for his soul. Later that night during meditation, I felt that he was less confused and was moving toward a much better place. The following morning when I meditated, I felt that Stan was at peace, yet he seemed to be in a very different loka from where my dad's soul had gone. I kept getting an image that he was in some sort of a spiritual hospital where his soul was resting in a structure that resembled a giant egg carton. He had now entered a place of healing and light that I can only attribute to Amma's grace. Several months later, I asked Amma if Stan's soul was at peace.

Before Mother responded to the question, she developed a far away look in her eyes for a few moments as if she were connecting with his soul and then she replied softly, "Don't worry about him. He's happy in the astral plane. Your niece, Rebecca, has nothing to worry about."

In contemplation on the deaths of my family members, an image arose in my mind. Every sentient being on Earth is holding a confirmed ticket to the astral plane. When we take a long trip to a foreign country, for example, we make reservations on a safe airline as well as at a comfortable place to stay when we arrive at our destination. Likewise, I realized that in preparing for my trip to the astral plane, I'll try to pay for my ticket to a divine loka through performing regular sadhana, selfless service and remembrance of God and Guru. Mother once told me that as long as I hold on to her feet, I would have nothing to worry about in the astral plane. God, please help me to constantly hold on to Amma's luminous lotus feet as I make my reservations for an eternal stay at Amma's Astral Inn.

Mother's advice for the devotee about the astral plane

I've always had a deep longing to know about what happens to my soul when I leave the body. I think some of the desire is based on fear that there may be suffering in the astral plane. As I previously mentioned, Mother rarely tells devotees about their past lives. It's very easy to get caught up in the glamorous maya of who "you" were in a past incarnation. Mother has frequently stated that the past is like a cancelled check. (Although if that's so, why does my check seem to be constantly bouncing back to my early childhood trauma?)

One time Swami Amritaswarupananda kept asking Amma about his past life. Mother finally acquiesced to his questioning by giving him a subtle hint about a possible incarnation the two of them shared. Swamiji told me that he couldn't even concentrate on singing bhajans because he kept thinking about that possible past incarnation. I have a friend who frequently explains events that are currently happening in his life solely on his belief of who he thinks he was in a past life.

In spite of realizing that it is futile to inquire about the astral plane, I still asked Amma recently, "I think a lot of my fear of death would be alleviated if Mother could share something about what happens when I leave the body so I won't be so frightened."

Amma responded, "It's no good to talk about the astral plane since unless you're at a higher state of being, you can't understand the subtleties of other worlds. Unless you're self-realized, you wouldn't understand the information and you would use the knowledge to enhance the ego. For example, the student of Vedanta will say that there is no astral plane; that everything is Brahman. The student of another path will argue with the Vedanta student stating that there is an astral plane."

How can any human with an ego possibly understand the subtle mysteries of the Universe? We are all just a speck within a speck within a speck. Our infinitesimal small minds think we have the audacity to really know what the Creator of the fathomless Universe is doing. It's like a baby flea sitting on the back of a gargantuan elephant interpreting why the massive mammal raises its trunk. All I can possibly do is to humbly develop my faith and devotion to the Holy Mother who will guide me to the goal.

CHAPTER VI

Mother heals my emotions

"If you are filled with anger, fear or jealousy, you will be a slave to those emotions. Whatever you think, do, or say will be colored by the negativity within you. How can you be free when you are bound by past regrets and by worries about the future? The emotions are like tenants. We have given them a small space to build a hut on our expansive land. Not only do they not care when we ask them to leave, they come to fight with us. We have to work to kick them out. We might have to argue in court also. Likewise, to kick out the tenants of the emotions we have to file a case in God's court. It is a constant fight. We must continue fighting until we come out victorious.

More vasanas come up as you do more sadhana. While sweeping a room, we can remove only the superficial dirt. Whereas, if the room is wiped with a wet cloth, more dirt will come out. In a similar way, more dirt will rise up when we do more sadhana. It is only for getting destroyed that they all rise up like that.

The mind creates such an itch when it is full of emotions. So you keep on scratching, until finally, your whole life becomes a big pus infected wound. All that pus needs to be squeezed out of your wound; only then will the wound be healed. It is Amma's duty to treat the wound and squeeze out the pus. That is how Amma shows Her compassion towards you."

Life in the Ashram

Mother always creates challenging situations for the devotees who choose to live in one of her ashrams. Mother once said that if you can live in Amritapuri, (her Indian ashram), you can survive anywhere in the world. Although the M.A. Center, Mother's ashram in California may not be as physically challenging as life in India, on an emotional level it can be quite intense. For my entire adult life I always had my own spacious house or apartment filled with all the accoutrements of the American lifestyle: large color television/ VCR; comfortable furniture; washer/ dryer; and beautiful artwork. I bought my favorite food items and prepared healthy meals when I wanted. If I didn't feel like washing the dishes after dinner, they would sit in the sink till the next day.

While I enjoy interacting with people, I am also a very private person and cherish my own quiet space. I knew there was no way I could ever live in a noisy, crowded ashram with my sensitivity to noise and stimuli.

Although I had asked Mother on several occasions if I could move into the ashram, I really had no intention of giving up my lifestyle or my beloved nine year old hound dog to live a Spartan life of tapas or austerities. In 1995, for some reason, I foolishly asked Amma again about the "possibility" of moving into the San Ramon ashram. A few days later several people came up to me and told me that they heard that I was moving into the ashram. Then Swami Paramatmanada walked up to me and said, "Dayalu, I heard that you're moving into the ashram."

I responded, "Who's going around spreading a ridiculous rumor like that?"

When he replied, "Mother told me," I knew I was in really big trouble.

Since Mother seemed to be-not so subtly- encouraging me to move into the ashram, I decided to compromise and look for a shared house near the ashram since I had been living three hours from San Ramon. I found a magnificent house near the M.A. Center with another devotee where I was able to bring my dog and all my material possessions. Strangely, within a few weeks of moving to San Ramon, I felt a powerful, magnetic force pulling me into the ashram.

Devotee meditating in front of the main house at the ashram

One morning a few months later, I suddenly woke up bewildered as I found myself looking around my new abode on the second floor of a tin barn in the ashram. Mother compassionately arranged a large living/work space that was ideal for me; nestled away in a room in the attic of a barn.

Once Amma hooked me into ashram life, she upped the ante, by creating a situation whereby I would have to move into a small, fifty-five square foot room next to a noisy kitchen in the dilapidated, one hundred fifty year old cottage on the ashram grounds with six roommates sharing one bathroom. In addition, I now had to move all of my remaining possessions out of my room twice a year when Mother came to San Ramon, since my room was used as the tour childcare room.

Mother has given me some interesting challenges to overcome such as: how to arrange my schedule to beat six ashramites to the bathroom every morning; how to tune out a conversation taking place in front of my door when I'm trying to sleep; and how to deal with the merry shouting of pre-school children under my window in the children's playground while conducting a vedic astrology reading.

I have found that nothing is impossible when I surrender to Amma. If someone had told me when I was living in my peaceful and comfortable two bedroom house perched on a magnificent, forested hillside a few years ago that I would be living under such austere conditions, I would have responded: "no way."

However, the more that the devotee opens up to Amma, the more she will peel away the disciple's vasanas so that only the divine remains. When I deeply contemplate on the truth that my body will soon become a pile of ash, I understand the absurdity of believing that my real happiness is dependent on living in a bigger house, obtaining a high paying job, or acquiring material possessions.

Living in the ashram with thirty-five people in such close proximity can create stress and tension. The small group of residents spend a great deal of time together eating, meditating, singing bhajans and doing seva. With so many people trying to complete numerous work responsibilities while working in small spaces, disagreements are naturally bound to arise.

Krishna told Arjuna in the Bhagavad Gita, "The devotee is dear to me who sees praise and blame as equal."

Mother creates challenging situations in the ashram for the devotee's spiritual benefit so the disciple will learn equanimity of mind. Nonetheless, in spite of the tense circumstances, Mother wants her devotees to treat each other in a loving manner.

I asked Mother once about the arguing that goes on during the ashram house meetings. Mother responded, "It's been bothering Mother for a long time how badly people treat each other during the house meetings. Mother has been meaning to do something about it so that people will treat each other with love. Even if someone speaks the truth, they shouldn't shame others."

On another occasion I asked Mother about disagreements that people were experiencing while trying to complete their seva. She stated, "There is fighting in the San Ramon ashram because some people want to be the king of their fiefdom and there is no love. As long as there is no love and people want to be king, there will be fighting. If there is love even in the ugliest place, there is beauty. People in the ashram are reacting from the mind, which is illusion, so how can there be peace of mind?"

Mother further stated on another occasion, "When Mother sees people hurting each other and then watches them come to her smiling and bowing, it makes her want to throw up. Doing seva, meditation and japa are totally worthless unless people can be loving and kind to each other."

However, Mother also told the ashramites that we should also have compassion toward people who do seva with an angry and negative attitude. She mentioned in a meeting with residents, "Everybody is not of the same caliber since some people have a troubled past. If you are really here to grow internally, then you should understand other people's drawbacks and shortcomings. You should understand that they are coming from a painful past and be compassionate toward them. That will help you as well as the other person grow spiritually."

Evidently, I need to develop my lack of compassion toward people who have had a painful past. I have found myself getting frustrated when I've observed some devotees abuse spiritual jargon just to strengthen their own ego. I remember when I asked another resident for help in moving some heavy boxes when I hurt my back, and he responded, "I'm not sure that helping you is the dharmic thing for me to do right now."

On another occasion I felt that one devotee was undermining a project that I was working on, so I asked her to be more supportive. She responded, "I'll have to meditate on that." At that point, I felt like yelling at her that all she needed to do was be more helpful instead of meditating.

However, with Mother's sage advice over the last few years, the residents began developing more equanimity of mind by treating each other in a kinder and more loving manner. With Amma's guidance and grace, the ashram meetings became more tranquil as residents began really listening to each other rather than immediately reacting from the ego.

Although most residents have been getting along better with each other, I asked Mother how to deal with discourteous people. I asked her if rude people should be told that they need to behave better, or should we just accept their abusive behavior?

Amma responded, "The highest way is to accept rude behavior. Things have gotten better amongst the way residents treat each other. You can't change someone else. It takes a long time for people to evolve."

Mother also once stated, "Only when you have the strength to withstand any ridicule and abuse heaped upon you, will Amma say that you are complete."

Mother later told me a story to help me how to learn to deal with difficult people. "When a man was a baby his mother changed his diapers and wiped his behind. The man now sees all rude people as his mother. By doing so, all negative people whom he meets are wiping his vasanas out. Patience with people is needed. Patience will take you to the goal, and when you're relaxed you can be more patient with people."

On another occasion when I told her that I found certain ashram residents' behavior intolerable, she wisely responded, "Everyone else in the ashram has problems. Instead of focusing on taking from people, if you concentrated on giving to the other residents, then perhaps they would change."

I meditated on Mother's wise advice and realized that I was making demands on others rather than focusing on what they needed. When I followed Mother's counsel by giving to my housemates, I experienced more harmony in the ashram.

It seems like Mother frequently puts people together who bring up each others emotional pain so that we will eventually learn detachment. When I commented to a Western devotee who lives in Amritapuri that it must be easier on a personal level in the Indian ashram since there are so many hundreds of residents, she responded that Mother will make sure that the one person out of a thousand who really irritates you will be in your face.

For a period of time I ended up living with another devotee who would constantly push my buttons and I would over-react by blaming him. We were both focusing on each other's negative qualities, which only served to augment the tensions between us. Even though we were no longer housemates due to our inability to get along, we both held on to a lot of anger toward each other. When I told Mother that I was not getting along with the other devotee, she responded, "The goal is to give up the ego. The jnani yogi thinks knowledge is the most important thing while the bhakti yogi believes that devotion is most important. Ultimately both types have to give up the 'I.' Therefore, you should forgive your former housemate. It is a good attitude to see any difficulties you experienced from him as your karma."

With Mother's grace and by my practicing forgiveness, I now feel no negative feelings toward the devotee who I had felt was my mortal enemy a few years earlier. As a matter of fact, I genuinely like the other person now, and it's hard for me to believe that we were once caught in an egotistic struggle. Today's enemy is tomorrow's friend and vice versa. Mother has taught me that the goal is to release attachment toward enemy or friend alike in this transient world of maya.

One of the most important answers Mother has ever given me to my questions on how to deal with difficult people happened

Dayalu and devotees celebrating Mother's birthday at the ashram

when I told her that I was at the end of my rope, and didn't know how to deal with my frustration with several devotees. She replied, "By getting to experience life in the ashram, eventually you will get disgusted with the pain and give up the battle." In retrospect, I understand how my identity was addicted to conflict, and with Mother's grace I have been able to begin to release the need to recreate negative emotional relationships.

When I truly accept and surrender to behavior towards me which I would normally consider offensive, I become detached and free. When I focus on the positive, I remember how even the most annoying people have exhibited kind and loving qualities at times. The more I can open my heart and refrain from judging others, the more love I feel toward all of my brothers and sisters in the ashram.

Sometimes devotees can develop a rather smug attitude about not wanting to be corrupted by associating with "worldly" people. Occasionally, I've heard disciples mention that they dread having to work outside the ashram with non-devotees. When I've resisted working with non-devotees, I've only demonstrated an attitude that is the antithesis of Mother's teachings of treating all beings with unconditional love and seeing God in all sentient beings.

I remember I judged an old friend for ordering a beer and a hamburger when we went out for dinner many years ago, which is exactly what I would have ordered before I became so "pure" now that I'm on a spiritual path. I also once asked a non-vegetarian devotee who lived in the ashram in a disdainful manner, "How can you eat dead animals?" However, I've come to learn that it's better to be a non-judgmental meat eater than a judgmental vegetarian. Ironically, a medical doctor recently told me that it would help my physical condition to eat some fish occasionally.

While it's true that sometimes it can be difficult for a devotee to be surrounded by people who are materialistically-oriented, use alcohol, drugs, or profanity, it's important not to judge non-devotees' behavior. Whenever I judge others' spiritual imperfections, I realize that I am just showing my lack of maturity.

I've observed malicious behavior amongst devotees who are supposedly trying to live a dharmic life, while I've seen some of the kindest and most compassionate behavior amongst non-devotees who are pursuing a "worldly life." Consequently, I asked Amma, "Can the billions of people on the planet who are living a compassionate and dharmic life without a Satguru have a chance to find God?"

Mother responded, "It is 10,000 times harder to find God without a Satguru, but if God sees the innocent longing of a person, he can find God. Just going to a Satguru is not enough. You need spiritual maturity to make any progress. There was once a scholar's parrot who had much wisdom, but an immature person ended up buying the bird and eating the parrot. Without maturity, just being with a Satguru is not enough."

After years of living in Mother's ashram, I am beginning to notice how she has changed me. I used to think other people's opinion of me was so important and wanted to interact with everyone to get their approval. I've learned that other people's opinion of me is none of my business, since everyone is just projecting their emotional issues onto other people.

Since I was not in the popular crowd when I was a boy in school, I had always wanted to meet someone from my past so that I could retroactively obtain the approval I wanted from my classmates. Through a series of uncanny circumstances, I recently met a man whom I went to school with thirty-five years ago. Steve, who was also from my Jewish, suburban New Jersey neighborhood, was very popular in high school and was now a leader of a Buddhist spiritual path. I nervously approached Steve after attending his Buddhist satsang one cold, November night last year. I felt hopeful that since we were both on a spiritual path, Steve and I would be able to connect on a spiritual level and I secretly hoped for his acceptance and approval.

However, Steve the Buddhist spent most of our discussion enumerating his many accomplishments in junior and senior high school, such as being on the basketball team and graduating in the top of our class, which brought up my old feelings of inadequacies. The meeting turned into a virtual Zen adolescent competition, as I tried to impress him with my post-high school athletic prowess and academic accomplishments. Although I really enjoyed seeing my old high school classmate, driving home that night I thought to myself, "I waited for over three decades to try to get approval from just another frail human with an inflated ego?" I realized how both of us spiritual men were stuck in our egos. Steve, the Buddhist from the "in crowd" was just as stuck in his ego as Dayalu, the Hindu from the "out crowd."

I understand that only Mother can give unconditional love. It's human nature for people to be your friend only if you can give them what they want; as soon as people aren't getting what they want from you, you're forgotten. By giving up the attachment of wanting mere mortals with egos to give me unconditional love, I now have developed a modicum of surrender and try to look to God for my source of eternal happiness.

Jealousy

Most devotees crave special love and attention from Amma. I remember quite a few instances when I would obsess on how another devotee received special attention from Mother, making me feel so jealous that I would not even be able to enjoy being in the presence of Amma. Once Mother told the devotees during a Rhode Island retreat, "One lady was sitting in front of Amma doing japa feeling Mother's bliss when she noticed another devotee giving Mother prasad. The woman suddenly became angry as she realized that the other person had already gotten to perform the coveted prasad seva twice and she hadn't been asked to do it at all. Mother then tried to talk to the jealous devotee and looked right at her for quite a while sending her much love, but the devotee couldn't even see or hear Amma since her jealousy and anger totally consumed her."

I came down with a case of jealousy when I noticed that Mother gave attention to other ashramites when she arrived in Seattle last year, but didn't say anything special to me. If the ashram bookstore sold an herbal remedy to antidote jealousy, Mother's charities probably could build homes for millions of poor people.

Throughout my stay in Seattle one year I kept obsessing how Amma never gives me any special energy. I didn't even notice that when she would climb the few steps to the stage every evening she would discreetly reach out her hand to lean on mine. I believed that she just needed the support to climb the stairs. One night I had to do seva when Amma ascended the stage, so I made sure another man was standing there to help her. Later, when I asked the other devotee how it went helping Amma onto the stage, he told me that he put out his hand, but she didn't lean on it.

Since most of the staff generally don't have much of an opportunity to spend time with Amma in the darshan hall, they frequently sit on the stage during the San Ramon evening programs. One night I noticed a man who pushed his way to the front of the stage and sat down right in front of one of the swamis during the evening talk. Although this "pushy" guy didn't seem to irritate the swami, I became quite jealous. I thought to myself, "Who does this guy think he is, anyway? I always see him sitting with Amma whenever I enter the temple throughout the day and now he takes over the space reserved for the staff. I'm going to tell that domineering guy that the stage is reserved for staff only... and not only that but he's blocking the view of a swami!"

However, I wasn't able to crawl over the other swamis to ask him to move that night. Since my seva had been working with the pre-teen children, I was fuming that I rarely get a chance to go to the evening programs, while this guy who never does any work, pushes his way to the front. Instead of concentrating on the uplifting talk about Amma, I was planning sophisticated methods of retaliation toward the pushy man.

Most devotees who come to see Amma enjoy doing various kinds of selfless service, such as serving in the kitchen or helping out in the hall. However, during the 2001 summer tour, no one would volunteer to help out with the pre-teen boys during the evening program, which I could understand. After all, if you had a choice of being in the "Temple of Divine Love" with Amma or watching the video "Temple of Doom" with twenty hyperactive boys, which would you choose?

The following night one of the pre-teen staff members sprained her ankle, but the seva coordinator reported that they still couldn't get anyone to volunteer to work with the boys during the evening program. That night as hordes of wild lads came charging into the pre-teen tent, to my chagrin the "pushy" guy who sat on the stage the previous night asked me if I needed any help with childcare. He turned out to be a godsend who worked well with the boys as well as being a really nice guy.

Mother is always creating situations so that the devotees can release jealousy. Amma once said during a satsang with the devotees "Maybe all my acts are to wake you up."

Mother's actions can be compared to putting rocks in a tumbler. After she shakes the rocks, the rough edges come off, making us polished pebbles.

During another tumbler special, I had an altercation with a devotee named Mike because I felt that he selfishly refused to move when he was blocking my view of Amma. I felt jealous that he's always in the hall with Amma, yet he wouldn't move over just a little bit so that I could look at Amma. In my egotistical reaction, I decided that I would never speak to him again for committing such a travesty against my spiritual development.

I was again feeling sorry for myself that I attended hardly any of the evening programs. However, I felt that I would be able to tune into Amma if I had an opportunity to do an extra lap seva shift whereby I could soak up her divine energy sitting close to her. I proceeded to make my request to the coordinator of lap shifts, who responded, "They are all filled for the rest of the time Amma is in San Ramon. However, since Mike has done a lot of shifts, you may want to ask him if you could replace him tomorrow."

I thought to myself, "Oh great, I have to ask my nemesis for a favor...like selfish Mike is really going to give up his chance of being near Amma for me."

Trying to get close to Amma makes even kind and thoughtful people act a little crazy. Although I was sure inconsiderate Mike would never give up his shift for me, I decided to ask him anyway which meant having to break my new rule of never speaking to him again. The ingrate responded, "I know that you don't get to be in the hall much so you can do my lap shift."

He added, "By the way, I'm sorry I didn't move over yesterday, but I was asked to sit there to help a disabled person who was going to need assistance going up for darshan." Ah, Mother burst yet another bubble in my never-ending stories of projection.

One ashram resident who is very mechanically inclined is a much better tractor driver than I am. One day a few years ago the ashram gardener asked me to do some tractor work but the priority for the tractor during that Saturday was completing a construction job. The expert tractor driver yelled for me to relinquish the tractor, but due to my immature jealously, I refused. In my dastardly attempt to maintain possession of the tractor, I drove too quickly into the garden knocking down the white, wooden gate. Not only did my childish jealousy result in destruction of the fence, but the mechanically-inclined resident was the person who repaired the fence, further aggravating my case of jealousy.

Amma, the embodiment of unconditional love, sees no real differences between any of the devotees. However, I frequently compare myself to people who are better than me. Mother told one devotee recently, "Don't compare yourself with those who are better off than you. Just because someone may have a nice car or big house doesn't mean that they are happy. Rather, you should compare yourself with those who are worse off than you."

She told one devotee recently who was feeling inferior to another devotee, "The attitude is important, not the type of work someone is doing. When Rama needed to get across the ocean to Sri Lanka and Hanuman threw in large boulders, did Rama love any less the squirrels that came and threw in pebbles?"

I asked Amma after the accident with the tractor, how I could release my jealous and addictive behavior of wanting to be accepted and approved by everyone. She replied, "You need to overcome your need to always get attention and approval from people. Mother will give you the strength to overcome this addictive behavior." She then added, "The vasana will slowly fade away in this lifetime."

Mother's sankalpa has miraculously helped me to release a lot of my jealousy. The following year, the proficient tractor driver told me that he needed to use the tractor while I was driving it, and I cheerfully acquiesced feeling no jealousy.

Later, during a dangerous and humbling incident, when the large, rented backhoe I was driving suddenly came to the verge of tipping over, one devotee screamed for me not to back up anymore! I hadn't driven the large backhoe in years and didn't know how to unlock the feet to stabilize the heavy piece of machinery that I was attempting to maneuver down a steep hillside. I asked one devotee to get the dexterous tractor driver. He rescued both the backhoe and myself from disaster. I then humbly acknowledged my ignorance in front of fifteen anxious spectators, feeling gratitude rather than jealousy.

Although I had been getting along well with this same resident whom I had previously been very envious of, in Seattle during the 2001 tour, old selfish thoughts started arising in my mind. After all the work I had done in letting go of envy, I didn't want to regress into a negative competition with him again. However, I felt helpless to stop the negative energy and was just about to make a rude comment.

However, later that same day I was swimming with the children in the indoor pool at the hotel when a devotee came running in and shouted that Mother requested that my former competitor and I give prasad together in a half hour. When we got next to Amma, he appeared very nervous and asked me to give prasad first. I felt a lot of empathy toward him when he showed his vulnerability and suddenly as we were kneeling next to Amma, all the jealous feelings simply evaporated. I understood that even if I did regress at times by feeling envious again, I knew that, with Mother's grace, I could once again overcome this negative emotion.

Learning detachment

I remember during one Devi Bhava program in Rhode Island many years ago there was an obnoxious person kneeling between Mother and the person who was receiving the sacred mantra from her. One devotee, Surya, who was in charge of asking people to leave the crowded stage, couldn't get the annoying fellow to move. Surya became more and more upset telling me that it was his last night with Amma and that the crazy guy was ruining the experience for him. I noticed that about an hour later, when Mother wanted the rude person to move, she told him to leave and he immediately left the stage. I've observed that Mother often has irritating people sitting close to her just to help the devotees learn detachment. I remember Swami Paramatmananda telling me that while not all of Amma's disciples will be liberated, they will all acquire a certain degree of *vairagya* (detachment).

Swami Paramatmananda and Amma in San Ramon

Swami Paramatmananda told a story about a guru in India who had a very obnoxious person living in his ashram who was making everyone angry. When the guru found out that the nasty person left the ashram, he ran after the ill-mannered disciple and offered to pay him to return to the ashram so that the devotees could keep learning the spiritual lessons of detachment and surrender.

Not only is Mother aware of all of our vasanas, but she understands the deep emotional causes of our behavior. Once I asked Mother about a devotee who was acting very rudely toward people in the ashram. Not only was Mother aware of this person's behavior, but she told me exactly when the person started behaving abusively toward others and why the person acted in such a discourteous manner. Amma added, "If you saw a crazy person in the street, it wouldn't bother you since you knew the person was insane. Likewise, you should see this person as crazy and not react."

I recently saw a bumper sticker that said "Don't believe your thoughts." One spiritual teacher wrote that thoughts are like having to spend time with a crazy relative who you know is insane. You can be gracious and hospitable to your crazy relative, but don't believe anything he says. Along the same lines, Amma once told me, "When you begin to constantly think, negativity arises and there is no end to it. If you do not think, there is no problem. Just float with the current."

Understanding projection

While Mother's grace is always present to help heal relationships, we also have to do some psychological growing up. I tried utilizing various techniques to help me heal an old pattern of feeling rejected and not being good enough. In my attempt to release anger toward people in the ashram, several years ago I began practicing a self-inquiry process of writing down my judgements about someone and then investigating the judgements by asking if they are true.

Through this process I learned that I didn't really meet anyone new, but I just kept creating the same situation with whomever I meet. I realized that it was more than a coincidence that I kept meeting pushy women and passive-aggressive men who reminded me of my parents. I was recently re-reading a letter I had written to someone with whom I was angry. I became disappointed with myself when I read how I was blaming the other person by collecting evidence on the terrible way she had treated me. However, to my utter dismay, when I finished reading the letter, I realized that the note was really written to another person.

When I accepted responsibility for my behavior by realizing that I possessed the quality that I didn't like in the other person, I was able to finally release my anger. For example, when I wrote out a list of all my judgements about an ashram resident who I thought acted selfish for ignoring me, I discovered the real truth: my thinking about the person was selfish since I was ignoring the other person's needs by egotistically focusing on myself.

I have come to realize that most people are projecting their beliefs onto others. I wish I had a dollar for every time someone told me that their type of counseling or spiritual path would have really helped me. Over the years, well-meaning friends have told me that I would finally be happy if I tried Freudian Psychoanalysis , Primal Therapy, EST, Co-counseling, Reichian, Bioenergetics, Gestalt and Rogerian therapies. Although some methods of counseling may work at times for some people, most of the techniques that friends urged me to try were ultimately a disaster since the modalities didn't resonate with my heart.

Concurrently, I notice how audacious I've behaved by urging others to join my therapy of the month club. I was just trying to validate my weak ego by showing people that I have found the cure for everyone's unhappiness. Ironically, I've had to acknowledge later that some of the techniques I had been urging others to try weren't even really that effective for myself. When the time was right, I found the perfect counselor on my own who helped me release old emotional pain. I remember one well-known counselor saying that whenever she was paid to visit someone in the hospital, she could never help the person because the patient wasn't ready.

Most devotees want all their friends and family to see their spiritual teacher thinking this teacher to be the highest. I've been cajoled into visiting more than fifty different spiritual teachers over the last twenty-five years, believing the projections of various devotees that their teacher was the only one who could help me find God.

Likewise, when I first saw Amma, I tried to bring everyone to see Mother. If anyone would dare to be so closed-minded that they would be reluctant to receive a blessing from Amma, I would become upset. However, I now understand that my acquaintances will receive the blessings of Amma through me, and that I'm the one who must remain open to understanding that each soul is like a flower which must bloom at a prescribed time. I acted like a fundamentalist preacher because I wanted others to validate my ego and affirm that I'm special because I have found the true path to God. When the student is ready the teacher appears. If it's not in someone's astrological chart to be with a certain spiritual teacher or even live a meditative life, how presumptuous of me try to change someone's karma.

The grip of maya is so strong that it feels like I'm constantly on the battlefield of *Kurukshetra* (site of the great war chronicled in the Indian epic,The Mahabharata), fighting the negative, untrue thoughts constantly arising in my mind. I certainly lost a battle with maya and projection when I rented a car with several devotees in Manhattan to drive to the Rhode Island retreat a few years ago.

The Manhattan car rental agent I dealt with appeared unscrupulous as he demanded in his loud New York accent, "Youse guys got a credit card?" As he puffed on his smelly cigar he continued, "I don't rent to nobody without no credit card." He then screamed at another customer, "I told ya to park da car over on thoity-foist street, not in dis here lot."

I was very nervous renting the car from this rather gruff and unpleasant man. On the drive back to New York by myself, I suddenly realized that the agent would try to illegally charge me for an extra day rental. During the four-hour trip, I created various scenarios in my mind as to how I would confront this dishonest clerk. I would tell him that my nephew is a local attorney who would sue him for his illegal actions and I would report him to the Chamber of Commerce as well as to the Better Business Bureau. I kept obsessing on what a jerk that rental agent was and how I shouldn't have rented from that crooked agency just to save a couple of bucks. With every mile I drove, I became more aggravated at the audacity of the agent who was trying to steal my money.

When I pulled into the parking lot on a hot, Sunday afternoon, I was really psyched to do battle with the ruthless car agent for taking advantage of me. As I nervously walked into the office, I kept rehearsing in my mind the script about how I was going to retaliate. I anxiously approached the counter. The salesman with the big cigar looked up at me and asked if everything went o.k. He checked the car and mileage and said thanks as he handed me my receipt.

What, no battle? I realized that I am an expert at making up stories about people that aren't true. The lies that were arising in my mind were the only instances of dishonesty in the rental transaction.

I still find self-inquiry very helpful in releasing anger. For example, when someone cuts me off while driving on the freeway, a thought arises, "what a stupid, dangerous driver. "

After I do the self-inquiry, I realize that I don't know why he cut me off. Maybe he's sick and trying to get to the hospital. I turn the false beliefs around by understanding that my own thinking about the driver was "stupid and dangerous."

While most of my projections have created conflicts, when I try to tune into the positive qualities of others, I create peace of mind for myself. Mother discussed in an informal satsang with ashram residents a few years ago the importance of focusing on the highest qualities. "Once there was a lot of unhappiness on earth. So Gods, Demons, and the humans went to Lord Brahma for a solution. Brahma just said 'Da.' The Gods thought it was the word 'daman,' meaning restraint. Gods are known for their extravagances so they followed Lord Brahma's word and started to control their senses and live accordingly. The demons thought it stood for the word 'daya,' meaning compassion. Demons, who are cruel by nature, started showing more compassion towards everybody. The humans interpreted the word as 'danam,' meaning donations, so they also obeyed Lord Brahma's command by giving to the poor. So peace and happiness prevailed throughout the three worlds. Likewise, the disciples should always look for the best in others."

Forgiveness heals emotional pain

As Amma told me once when I was trying to release my anger toward one ashram resident, "The entire problem is all in the mind. A man was in a dark room, fighting on and on until he finally turned the light on and realized there was no one there. He was just fighting himself." I meditated on what Amma told me and finally realized that the peace that I seek will never be found with the mind, so I must align with the divine.

Mother also shared with me more sage advice when I told her that I seemed unable to release my anger. "Understanding and realizing your anger are different things. Your anger affects you just like oil that is poured into an empty tube. Things will get stuck and there will be no flow. You can't get close to Amma because of your anger. It's the attachment that's creating the anger. Once the pain becomes unbearable you will drop it. The anger is poisoning you, not hurting other people. Other people may not even know about your anger."

Amma confirmed what I had written twenty years earlier for my doctoral dissertation. Anger is the most important feature of the Type A personality that creates coronary heart disease. When we get angry, adrenaline is pumped into the arteries that keeps the cholesterol stuck, preventing the blood from flowing to the heart.

Although Mother created situations for me in the ashram that would bring up my rage from my childhood, I felt that deep-seated pain from many incarnations were going to be finally released. While letting go of my anger and sadness has been a painful process, I remembered Mother has frequently told the devotees that a mahatma is like a doctor who has to squeeze the pus out of a wound which momentarily creates pain, but the treatment results in the patient being healed.

In my attempt to cut out my anger using Mother's scalpel, I listened to a tape on forgiveness. I listened to one cassette continuously, meditating on the words, "Forgiveness opens the doorway to love and sets us free. When we refuse to forgive we sit in a prison of self-righteous resentment. We stay stuck in the past which only hurts ourselves. The other person may not even know that we are in pain."

The tape continued, "Visualize letting go of past hurt and suffering. Look at the painful incident from the other person's perspective. That person was only mirroring what you believed to be true about yourself. Now let all the old pain dissolve and disappear. Set the other person free and set yourself free. I forgive everyone and I forgive myself. I am free. I am free."

After several weeks of deeply praying to Amma, listening to the forgiveness tape and practicing self-inquiry, I felt something deep within me shift and I was no longer angry at some of the ashram residents whom I previously had a difficult time forgiving.

I've noticed that when I'm not able to forgive, it's because I don't want to give up the need to be abused. A counselor once told me that people usually don't let go of their emotional pain because they are so attached to it that they'd rather die than give up the wound.

However, having studied the techniques that can help me grow emotionally and spiritually, it is important for me to start living the teachings. Another teacher whom I saw many years ago asked the audience, "How many people realize that making value judgements about other people is harmful to you as well as to others?"

Virtually everybody in the room raised their hand. Then she asked, "How many people in the audience still judge other people?" Again, virtually everyone in the room raised their hand. The teacher then yelled out, "Stop it now. Stop it now. Stop it now." That experience helped me to understand how important it is to remember to implement all the positive spiritual and emotional techniques that I've learned right now. There is a difference between believing the truth and living the truth.

I recently had a stimulating discussion at the beginning of a walk with a friend of mine, Nandita, about the importance of not judging anyone, investigating the thoughts arising in the mind and focusing on the present moment. We then shared how much we both enjoyed several different books on these subjects and that we've recommended these books to our friends. I then discussed with Nandita what Mother has told the ashram residents about the importance of not judging others and observing the thoughts in the mind.

We both acknowledged what a blessing it was that we had so many techniques available to help us grow spiritually and emotionally. I then expressed empathy for all the people who aren't on a spiritual path and were stuck in negativity not knowing how to change.

As our exhilarating walk through the hilly forest came to an end, I suddenly realized that for the last hour of the trek, we had both been complaining about people, situations and events as well as expressing fear of the future. I felt quite dismayed when I realized that, for all my new age banter, I still hadn't begun living the truth. However, I felt somewhat consoled when I recalled what Amma told me many years ago: that I needed to be patient since it's very hard to dissolve the ego.

Be a witness to the thoughts

Mother's grace helped me to investigate my projections as well as forgive people in order to release my anger and sadness. A third technique that I have found very helpful in releasing negative emotions is being the witness to thoughts arising in the mind. Mother once discussed with the ashram residents the importance of observing the mind. She said, "Trying to harness the mind is like trying to catch the wind. It is difficult to have just one thought. So try to understand the nature of the mind and just be a witness to your thoughts."

Mother continued, "Anger is a very strong emotion so it may take some time to understand the nature of anger. You should be patient and analyze the situation that made you angry. You should move away from the situation that caused the anger. Neither reject or accept the rage… just remain awake and try to witness the whole situation."

When I observe my thoughts, I visualize myself standing at a bus stop watching the destination signs on top of the buses passing by. Here comes a bus that says "worry about my health"... that one says "be concerned that I don't have enough money"... and here's a motor coach travelling to "I feel lonely without a relationship." Finally, I see a bus in the far-off distance that seems to have a sign bathed in a luminous, white light with the destination "to the heart of Amma." I think I'll catch that coach!

While writing this book, I began to feel that I had actually made some emotional and spiritual progress since moving into the ashram. However, the ego, which thrives on separation and conflict, was determined to disturb my newfound tranquility. I recently began obsessing on old childhood emotional pain, which felt like quite a setback for my soul and a victory for the ego. While the ego definitely is ahead in points in this incarnation, with Amma's grace, the soul could still be victorious in the final quarter.

One morning I prayed deeply to Amma to help rid my mind of old, negative thoughts that were beginning to take hold of my consciousness again. That afternoon I received a letter from the library stating that a requested book had arrived.

The book dealt with the power of staying in the present by observing thoughts. This idea motivated me to try to spend the next week observing my thoughts. As soon as I realized that I was fixating about a morose, past event, I was instantaneously put in the present, which seemed to help dissolve the negative emotion. As I consciously practiced being aware in the moment through observing thoughts, I noticed that all my problems dissolved. I felt like the stillness of Being was finally beginning to be victorious over my ego/mind. I remembered that the word "now" spelled backwards is "won" (one).

When I became aware that I was worrying about having to move all my possessions out of my tiny room for Amma's

November visit, I just sat in the present and observed the radiant, yellow leaves falling from the trees on the crisp, clear Fall day. I gazed at the luminous sunlight streaming through my windows before dusk. I enjoyed feeling Amma's compassionate eyes filling me with her effulgent love from the large Devi Bhava picture on top of my altar. I then closed my eyes and began focusing on different parts of my body, feeling divine energy flowing through me. When a worry arose, I observed, "that's a fearful thought about the future"... and returned to the present. Although the ego still sends incessant, negative thoughts about the past and future, I feel that there is a power within me that is able to dissolve the negativity and experience the bliss of the present.

A healing between father and son

Sometimes we need a mediator to help us heal a wounded relationship. By the summer of 2001, my relationship with my adult son, David, had really deteriorated. I wanted to improve the connection and asked Amma in San Ramon to bless us that my son and I would have a healing. She told me that she would bless the healing. I arranged for us to meet with a counselor when I visited him in Boulder, Colorado. I found the best time in both of our astrological charts to heal the conflict. There was a period of only four days after Amma left San Ramon that was very auspicious for a healing.

With Amma's grace, a very auspicious date and a willingness of both people to change, I arranged two sessions with a counselor, who turned out to be one of the most competent therapists I've ever met. The counselor asked both of us to tell the other what they didn't like about the relationship. We were only allowed to acknowledge what the other person said by repeating back the statements rather than defending ourselves.

Then we were asked to tell the other person that we could understand how a certain behavior would bother him. For example, David said that he could understand that when he avoids contacting me, I would become angry because it would remind me of how I felt rejected when I was a boy in school.

My son David and Dayalu

During the second session, the counselor asked both of us if we have ever reacted in the same manner with anyone else. Naturally, I had to admit that I have gotten upset with many people when I believed that they were rejecting me. David acknowledged that he had recently avoided interaction with his mom when he mistakenly thought that she had criticized him. By each of us taking responsibility for our core issue, the other party felt that the defensive reactions weren't personal.

The counselor then asked David how he felt when he was being criticized and how I felt when I believed I had been rejected. The proficient therapist was able to help us accept our core issues. David told me that he feels worthless when he's criticized, so he avoids those painful feelings by withdrawing from people who criticize him. The counselor then asked David if he would be willing to acknowledge the feelings that he had been avoiding his entire life. I felt tears running down my cheeks as my competent and powerful son painfully admitted his hidden feelings of vulnerability and worthlessness by repeating "I'm worthless."

I told my son that I feel that I'm disgusting when I think that I'm being rejected and that I criticize him to avoid feeling the repulsive shadow part of myself. The therapist then asked me to repeat the words, "I'm disgusting"... the feelings that I, too, have been afraid to acknowledge.

Even with a Ph. D. in psychology and ten years of therapy, I found it very difficult to express my weaknesses. However, as I continually said, "I am disgusting," I began feeling the pain deeply in my body. Suddenly, I felt a deep release from the core of my being, setting me free. Once I accepted my inadequacy and realized that I wasn't going to be permanently damaged by owning that part of myself, a deep healing occurred. I don't think that I could be upset in that way with my son anymore now that I understand that his avoidance of me has less to do with me and more to do with his avoiding his feelings of worthlessness. Likewise, if I should become critical of David if he avoids me, he will be more understanding that my criticism has nothing to do with him, but is based on my avoiding feeling disgusting. Thank you Amma for blessing this parent-child healing and opening my heart.

CHAPTER VII

Faith in Amma

"Spirituality is faith. Only complete undivided faith can help one reach the goal.

One who has faith (sraddha) *will never swerve from the path.*

If you don't have strong faith in Mother, doubts will crop up in your mind regarding Mother's actions. You may feel, 'Why is Mother talking to that person for such a long time and not even looking at me?' Such doubts will create many obstacles in your spiritual path due to your seeing only the external Mother. This will not happen if you enshrine Mother within. You must also have the strong conviction that 'Mother is not the body, but the all-pervading Consciousness.'"

THE FIRE

On Monday night, June 13, 2000, I felt that I was coming down with a flu. When I awoke Tuesday morning I had a fever, my muscles ached and I felt totally exhausted. I decided that I would rest all day in a small isolated place in the back of the property since I had no room during the tour. As the day progressed, my fever became higher, but I became too exhausted to move. Suddenly, something that sounded like a sonic boom woke me up, but strangely I quickly fell back to sleep. A little later, I kept being disturbed by the loud noises of helicopters overhead, but again, I kept falling back asleep. Several hours later I walked to the dining structure to find out why there were so many helicopters flying overhead. To my shock and dismay, I was told that a propane tank exploded and seven people were severely burned and airlifted to hospitals. There was a possibility of the wind spreading the fire, so many of the devotees were evacuated from the area. I later learned that if the fire had spread in a Western direction, I would have been trapped in the woods in the rear of the ashram where I had been resting.

Mother was watching the fire from the balcony at Ron's house near the ashram. I feel that her intervention created many miracles that day which otherwise could have caused a major catastrophe. When the devotees were seriously burned in the fire, some people wanted to immediately put them in the pond. Fortuitously, an emergency medical technician happened to be at the site of the fire and wouldn't let the devotees soak the burn victims in the water. If they were bathed with pond water, they could have developed a fatal bacterial infection from the impure water.

After the initial explosion in the kitchen tent, the fire began rushing toward the woods near two barns that would have instantaneously shot up in flames. However, the wind abruptly shifted, as the fire returned toward the dining hall, but then suddenly went up a hill toward a major freeway, route 680. However, even before the firemen arrived, witnesses stated that the fire miraculously stopped in its tracks and simply died down.

A few days later when I walked along the fire route, I was truly amazed. The fire path ran parallel less than a foot from the dining structure but never burnt the dining hall (except for one corner that occurred during the initial explosion). However, what really surprised me was that the fire literally stopped inches in front of a huge propane tank that was located behind the dining structure, and suddenly turned up the hill. If the large propane tank exploded, the devastation to both people and the property could have been catastrophic. Although the report of the fire was listed on the front page of many of the local newspapers as well as on the local television stations, the media reports were not pejorative toward Amma or the ashram.

An earlier fire at the ashram in the early '90's. Due to a lack of rain during the summer in California, there is a constant danger of fire.

All seven of the burn victims who were hospitalized exhibited so much faith in Amma. The hospitalized men were in better shape than the women due to the fact that the ladies were wearing saris which spread the flames. The burn victims were in surprisingly such good spirits, despite the fact that they were in pain with seared skin over much of their body.

I visited the hospitals where these patients were recovering a few days after the fire. As I put a picture of Amma into each of their charred hands that were wrapped tightly in gauze, each devotee would gaze at the picture lovingly for a few moments with much devotion and love. Tears welled up in my eyes as I felt their deep abiding faith in Mother. When I visited the most severely burned patient who was hooked up to life support systems, she squinted up at me and bravely whispered, "Tell Amma not to worry about me."

Mother had warned some devotees of the danger of fires a few weeks earlier before she departed India for the world tour. She also mentioned that all the people who were injured in the fire were destined to have had a traumatic incident happen to them that day, but because it happened in the ashram with Amma nearby, the severity was reduced. Amma also told one of her close devotees right before the fire started that she saw something very ominous was going to happen that day. When she expressed her vision, the disciple told her to rest and not to worry.

Niramayan, a joyful Brazilian man who loves to cook for the devotees, related that for just about an hour after he was severely burned, he questioned how Mother could have allowed the fire to happen. He said that his mind briefly went into a state of darkness. However, while still in the emergency room, his negativity and anger toward Amma was totally transformed, and he suddenly emerged into being totally at peace. Although he experienced the pain of his blistered body, he felt Mother came to him, and amazingly his mind became filled with joy. Niramayan mentioned that he was only able to deal with the severe pain because he felt Mother was with him. Upon his immediate arrival at the burn unit of a local hospital, he had to be bathed to scrape the dead tissue and clean the wounds. Although this procedure was excruciatingly painful, Niramayan continuously sang the bhajan, "Aye Guru Maharini." The words to the song mean "Amma, self-realized master, protect us and give us refuge."

Mother had previously told the devotees in a satsang, "By loud singing to God, one can overcome distracting sounds and achieve concentration."

Although the pain was almost unbearable, by singing very loudly with all his heart, the brave devotee transcended the agony as the doctors scraped his freshly charred skin. Niramayan related that although his body continued to experience pain, he was feeling incredible peace of mind when he was hospitalized. He was living in his heart and accepting that everything that was happening to him was coming from God.

Niramayan also mentioned that the physical suffering helped him to grow closer to God. When other people told him that they didn't think that they could have maintained his positive spirit if they had been severely burned, Niramayan responded, "Mother would never forsake her devotees. Her infinite grace and compassion will always be there, no matter what happens or what experiences we go through. She will find a way to bring us into the heart."

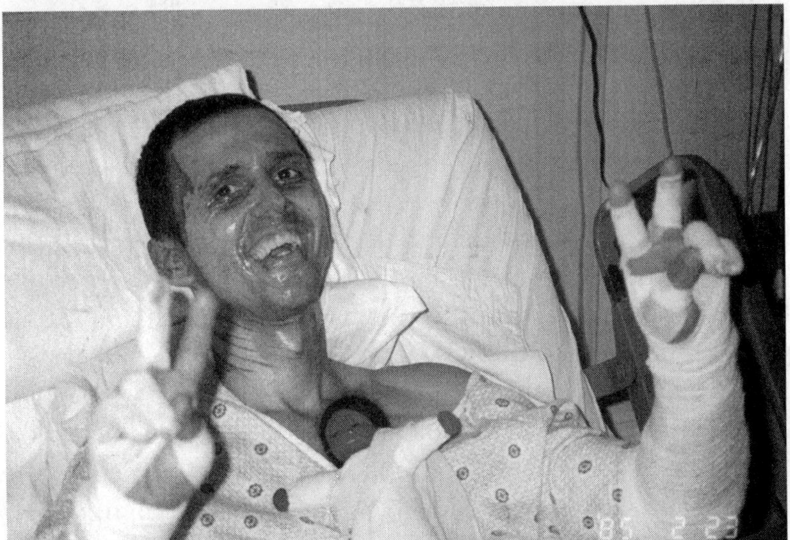

Niramayan experiencing Mother's bliss while recovering in the hospital

A few days after the fire, when Mother visited Niramayan and the other patients in the hospital, she expressed so much sadness upon seeing her children suffering. However, Niramayan told her, "Mother, after some time these wounds will be healed and the pain will be gone. This is all impermanent. But to have permanent devotion towards you is so rare and difficult. The mind always gets in the way. Please bless me with devotion."

Mother responded, "The planetary system hasn't been favorable. This was bound to happen. This is a test. It was good that the accident happened at Mother's ashram. If you are able to surrender to this moment, you'll be stronger. Now is the time to have faith and surrender."

Have Faith in the Guru

Mother further stated in a meeting she convened with the ashram residents right after the fire, "Many things happen around a master. In Mecca, the holiest place for the Muslims, there are fires and accidents that happen annually. Many thousands of people died but still every year more people go to Mecca. Nobody is losing faith. A few years ago a famous church built by St. Francis was in an earthquake and the church collapsed. Some people died there, but nobody lost faith."

"We should look at things positively. The fire happened. But it is better that this did not happen when thousands of people were there. Otherwise it would have been a disaster."

Amma further elucidated the topic of faith by stating, "We should look at the Masters… at how they are helping the world. That is the practical way of looking at things. Some people become afraid when some devotees leave the ashram thinking, 'what will happen to me?' If there are a hundred people in an ashram some will naturally leave and new people will come. If we focus on the people who leave the ashram, we will become unsteady. Remember the disciple is not perfect. He has come to the guru to become a perfect person. If we only look to a disciple (no matter how advanced he may be), it is like walking with a stick. If the stick is gone you will not be able to walk. Look toward the guru and observe how the guru lives."

During another discussion, she illustrated some priceless analogies to teach the devotees the importance of focusing on the guru rather than the disciple. "Even if disciples are with Mother for twenty or thirty years, it doesn't mean anything. It's like a frog living under a lotus flower, eating only mud, or, like a ladle stirring the sweet pudding year after year. After you wash the large spoon, it doesn't taste any sweeter. Under the lighthouse, it's always dark. A mosquito on the udder of a cow gets only blood, not milk. However powerful a guru is, the situation is like a radio station. It doesn't matter how powerful the radio station is, if a person's radio is not on."

Considering the horrendous state of events in the world today, it seems to me that most of the problems on the earth can be traced to disciples following the distorted ego of a follower of a master rather than focusing on the guru's teachings. Likewise, if one puts all the disciples in one room they would agree on nothing, but if you put all the masters in one room they would agree on everything.

I notice that when I focus on the negative, I lose faith and cease to develop spiritually. I remember one spiritual teacher state that we could be looking at one of the most beautiful rugs in the world, but if we are focused on negativity, we would choose to see only the imperfection of one little thread misplaced in an otherwise magnificent tapestry.

The ego thrives on separation and negativity to maintain its separate identity from God. Therefore, it is important to focus our attention on the divine teachings of the guru and keep our faith, no matter what calamities seem to occur in the illusory world of maya. If we hold on to the guru's feet with faith and love throughout all of life's raging storms, we will ultimately arrive safely on the shore of eternal peace.

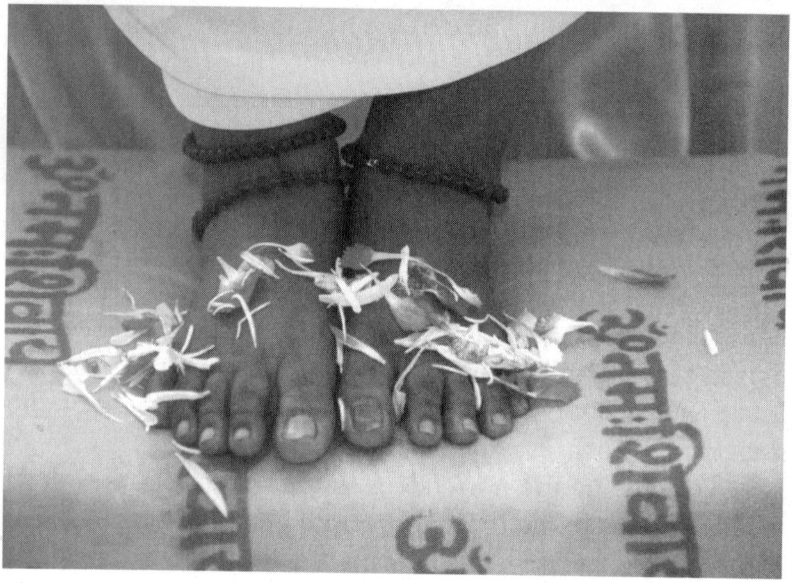

The terrorist attack

Mother told some disciples that she had a dream the night before the terrorist attacks in the United States. In the dream she saw an elephant attacking her. She further stated that this was a very bad omen. Even before the tragic events began to unfold on September 11th, Amma did not apply the *tilak*, a mark of kukum and sandalwood powder on the forehead. Omitting this mark is customary for people who are in mourning. By chance, Swami Ramakrishna arrived in Manhattan the day before the tragedy to give a satsang. Mother called him up right before the tragedy occurred to see how he was doing.

In Amritapuri many of Amma's children from the United States approached Mother in tears upon learning about the disaster. Amma cried with them. She repeatedly asked the devotees to pray. Mother also instructed the residents in Amritapuri to perform special pujas for the departed souls, chant the thousand names of the Divine Mother, and repeat mantras for world peace. Continuous archanas dedicated to world peace and for the victims and families of the tragedy were also conducted at the M.A. Center in San Ramon.

Mother sent the following message to her children throughout the world: "My darling children, Amma understands that a lot of innocent lives were lost. At this critical time, the leaders, and we also, need to practice discrimination and self-restraint. If we do not do so, many more lives will be lost. We should all sit down and pray for the welfare and peace of the whole world. This is how we can help all of our brothers and sisters."

During a satsang in Amritapuri a few days after the tragedy, Mother discussed the world crises. "It was the prarabdha (destiny) of those people who died for them to go like ripe leaves on a tree. When an eagle lands on a tree suddenly all the leaves drop. A huge bird makes the leaves shed, but they were ready to fall. Their souls left the body but the *Atman* (spirit) is eternal. Amma is worrying about their near and dear ones who are suffering. We can pray that everyone perform good actions so nobody suffers in the future.

"There is a lot of anger boiling inside the citizens of America because the buildings attacked were their signs of prosperity. America was the most powerful nation in the world, yet this happened. This shows that we can find true refuge only in God.

"We needn't blame a nation or religion. Some people have fanatic attitudes. If a doctor gives medicine that is wrong for the patient, you cannot blame the company that manufactures the medicine, only blame the doctor who gave the wrong prescription."

The following day in an informal satsang Amma added, "Amma feels particularly sad right now thinking about those innocent people who were charred when the plane crashed into those buildings. Amma feels immensely sad when she thinks about all the children who lost their parents, the parents who lost their children, the sisters and brothers who lost their siblings. And think of how many husbands lost their wives, and how many wives lost their husbands. Amma feels so tremendously sad and her heart reaches out to those who are going through all that agonizing pain caused by that terrible, destructive act. My children, let us all pray for the peace of the departed souls and the quick recovery of those who were injured, and for the welfare of all beings in the world. May the *Paramatman* (the Supreme Being) bless everyone with enough strength to overcome their grief, and may the dark forces of negativity and ignorance give way to the light, love and peace of God."

Although Mother had said in her message that we should pray for peace, she also said it was important to practice self-restraint. Therefore, in discussions with friends, I mentioned that it could be dangerous to attack a foreign country at this time. I advocated a method similar to how the Israelis captured the nazi fugitive Adolph Eichman in Argentina in 1961 without harming any innocent people.

During dinner one night in the ashram, I mentioned my opinion regarding a restrained policy toward capturing the terrorists and another devotee emphatically stated that Mother said we should only pray. When I tried to explain that my position was based on what Mother mentioned about self-restraint, I was told that that was my interpretation of what Mother said. He reiterated that we are only supposed to pray. As the discussion became more heated, I told him that he sounded like a fundamentalist. Everyone should follow only Mother's exact words without voicing an opinion. As the two of us became angrier with each other, it didn't appear that either one of us were following Mother's teachings of restraint or understanding as we both became so engrossed in proving the other person wrong.

Suddenly I realized that we were exhibiting terrorist attitudes toward each other, shooting off lethal words of poison. We both finally calmed down, and tried to understand what had just happened. Although we resolved the conflict, I felt a sense of hopelessness that if two devotees living in an ashram could so easily express terrorist and fanatic attitudes toward each other, what hope was there for the world? I then remembered my days in the anti-Vietnam War movement where we hypocritically fought for peace. Outer peace is only a reflection of inner-peace.

By turning off the news media, which only reinforced my fear and anxiety, and by praying to Mother, I finally calmed down and began to feel hopeful. I couldn't have possibly stayed detached and centered when I was constantly hearing the tortuous stories of thousands of grieving families and watching our tallest buildings collapsing. Imagine how horrific it would have been if there were CNN broadcasts during World War II at the invasion of Normandy, at the concentration camps and at Hiroshima? I finally understood that praying, maintaining silence and developing faith in God were my only means available for creating both inner and outer peace.

Although Mother is omniscient and aware of everything that is going on in the world, she rarely reveals specific information, except occasionally in the form of subtle hints. When Mother cancelled one of the programs in Europe after the September 11th tragedy, one devotee asked Amma, "What can we do now? I am so nervous that something may happen and the planes may stop flying and you may not come."

Amma responded, "Know that when you are born you have to die one day. This is the nature of life. But when death comes, we should be ready to accept it with a smile. We should be prepared for this. We cannot live in this world by being nervous or anxious about the future.

"God himself tried to change the world and has not been successful. In fact when incarnations like Christ, Mohammed Nabi and Krishna came unto earth, there was so much killing. So do not get nervous. God's creation is full of happiness and it is our creation that is full of sorrow. Just as a child who feels supported by the mother plays happily, we should be happy in the world knowing that God and guru are there to take care of us."

While I noticed a few weeks before the tragedy that from an astrological perspective, it was going to be very inauspicious for me personally, I didn't realize how the magnitude of the planetary configuration would affect the world. While it is comforting to understand astrologically why certain inauspicious events occur, the only real comfort I felt during the tragedy was praying to God and Amma for peace and harmony. Even if peace prevails throughout the world, in one hundred years virtually all beings who are currently living on the Earth plane will have left their bodies. As Mother said in her birthday message in October 2001, "When we are born into this world we do not bring anything with us. When we go, we cannot take anything. Should we fill our short lives with jealousy, hatred and greed? Only the merit of selfless actions that we have performed will accompany us on our final journey."

Therefore, it seems clear that our only hope for eternal joy during either peaceful or catastrophic times is to incessantly pray to Amma and God, repeat our mantra, sing bhajans with devotion, serve others lovingly and maintain an awareness of the temporary nature of the world.

When I meditate deeply on the following verses of Mother's sacred words from the song "Omkara Divya Porule," my soul experiences profound eternal hope, peace, and joy.

Children, do not encourage egotistic competitiveness to grow within you.

Let the awareness of the oneness of the Self grow in every situation and let that be your constant companion.

Dedicate yourself to the mission of uplifting those who are less fortunate than you.

*

To be proud of the body and the power of the senses-how pathetic that is! Alas, the body will decompose back into its constituent elements one day.

*

The deep ocean far from the shore is calm and peaceful. But its waves near the shore are restless. The mind immersed in meditation is at peace; that which is trapped in its emotions is turbulent.

*

Children, pray for the welfare of even those who heap abuse and blame on you. The mind should have the strength to forgive when anger rises up.

*

A lot of people may sing our praises and a lot of people may condemn us. If we have confidence in our own selves, both of these are equal to us.

*

The past is dead and buried, the future is beyond the hand's reach. The present is in our control; whatever is to be gained, we should gain right now.

*

The God that you are seeking, all the while imagining that He is far away, dwells so close to you. He stands right beside you in a human form full of compassion, waiting for your recognition.

*

Children, seek God like babies who hang on to their mothers' aprons, never letting go, and constantly plead for attention.

*

Mother will bring you up as her darlings. She will clear your path in each step. If you take in the meaning of her words and go forward, she will open your mind's eye.

Om lokaha samasthaha
sukhino bhavantu

May all beings in the universe
be happy

Glossary

Adharma: Unrighteous behavior

Amrita: Divine nectar

Avatar: Incarnation of God

Archana: Recitation of the names of the Divine Mother

Asanas: Hatha yoga postures

Ashram: The home of a group of people who lead a spiritual life; generally the home of a spiritual teacher

Atman: The Eternal Self; God

Ayurveda: The ancient healing system of India

Bhajan: Devotional singing

Brahmacharya: A celibate spiritual aspirant

Darshan: Audience of a holy person

Devi Bhava: Divine mood or identity with the Goddess; the Divine Mother

Devotee: One who has faith in God or a specific saint

Dharma: Righteous behavior in accordance with Divine Harmony

Divine Mother: A manifestation of God in the feminine form

Dosha: physical constitution

Guru Poornima: An auspicious annual holiday honoring the guru during the full moon

Hari Bol: Chant the name of God

Harmonium: An organ-like keyboard instrument with small metal reeds

Jai: Victory
Japa: Repeating a mantra
Ji: Used as a form of respect at the end of a name
Kali: Goddess of destruction and transformation
Krishna: Incarnation of Lord Vishnu
Krishna Bhava: Divine mood or identity with Krishna
Kurukshetra: Battle site from the Bhagavad Gita
Leela: Divine play
Loka: World
Mahasamadhi Mandir: Site where a saint consciously left his body and merged into God
Mahatma: Great soul
Mantra: A sacred syllable or phrase
Mata: Mother
Mata Amritanandamayi: Ammachi's formal name; mother of immortal bliss
Maya: Power of universal illusion that makes the world seem real
Moksha: See Realization
Pitta: Fire constitution in Ayurveda
Prarabdha: Karma; Action seen as bringing upon oneself inevitable results either in this life or previous births
Pranam: To bow with folded hands
Prasad: Sacred offering, usually food
Puja: Ritual worship, ceremony
Punya: Merit

Rajasic: Hyperactive, restless
Realization: The state of complete identity with God
Sadhak: A spiritual seeker
Sadhana: Spiritual practices
Samadhi: State of absorption in God
Sankalpa: Resolve
Sannyasin: A renunciate monk
Satguru: Realized spiritual master
Satsang: Spiritual gathering; spiritual discourse by a saint or scholar
Sattvic: Harmonious
Self: God; one's spiritual essence not identified with body or mind
Seva: Selfless service
Sevite: A devotee performing selfless service
Shraddha: Awareness, faith
So hum: Sanskrit for God and I are one
Sri Chakra: The Universal Mother
Tamasic: Low energy; dull
Tapas: Spiritual austerities
Tilak: Kukum and sandalwood powder on the forehead
Vairagya: Detachment
Vasanas: Latent ego tendencies of the mind resulting from prior actions
Vata: Air constitution in Ayurveda

BIBLIOGRAPHY

Amritaswarupananda, Swami, *Awaken Children, Volumes I-VII; Dialogues with Mata Amritanandamayi* , San Ramon, Ca. M.A. Center, 1995

Bhjajanamritam: Devotional Songs Vol.3, San Ramon, CA. M.A. Center, 1996

Byron Katie, *The Work of Byron Katie*, Los Angeles, The Work of Byron Katie Foundation, Inc., 2001

Hay, Louise, *You Can Heal Your Life*. Los Angeles, CA., Hay House, 1984

Millay, Edna St. Vincent, *My Candle Burns At Both Ends*, *The Treasury of American Poetry*, Garden City, New York Guild America Books, 1978

Tolle, Eckhardt, *The Power of Now*, Novato, Ca. New World Publishing, 1999

Yogananda, Paramahansa, *Cosmic Chants*, Los Angeles, Ca.: Self-Realization Fellowship, 1974

Zeff, Ted, *Searching For God: A Journey into the Heart of the Divine Mother Part I*, San Ramon, Ca.: Shiva Publishing, 1997

RESOURCES

FOR INFORMATION ABOUT OTHER BOOKS ON AMMACHI, CONTACT:

AMMACHI PUBLICATIONS
P.O. BOX 613
SAN RAMON, CA 94583
TEL. 510-537-9467
www.mothersbooks.org

You may also order books about Amma from your local bookstore

FOR INFORMATION ABOUT AMMACHI TOURS: VISIT www.ammachi.org OR CALL 510-537-9417

UNITED STATES ASHRAMS AND CENTERS:

There are Ammachi satsang groups that meet regularly in 42 cities in 20 states throughout the United States as well as in 5 cities in Canada. Please call the M.A. Center in San Ramon, California at 510-537-9417 for information regarding local Ammachi groups in North America or visit the web site: www.ammachi.org

INDIA ASHRAM AND CENTERS THROUGHOUT THE WORLD:

For information about Ammachi satsang groups in other countries and Mother's ashram in India please visit the web site www.amritapuri.org

